THE ARTHUR YOUNG PRACTICAL GUIDE TO INFORMATION ENGINEERING

THE ARTHUR YOUNG PRACTICAL GUIDE TO INFORMATION ENGINEERING

ARTHUR YOUNG
INFORMATION TECHNOLOGY GROUP

JOHN WILEY & SONS

New York   •   Chichester   •   Brisbane   •   Toronto   •   Singapore

This publication is designed to provide accurate and
authoritative information in regard to the subject
matter covered. It is sold with the understanding that
the publisher is not engaged in rendering legal, accounting,
or other professional service. If legal advice or other
expert assistance is required, the services of a competent
professional person should be sought. *From a Declaration
of Principles jointly adopted by a Committee of the
American Bar Association and a Committee of Publishers.*

Action Diagrammer®, Dataflow Diagrammer™, Decomposition
Diagrammer®, Entity Diagrammer®, GAMMA™, Information
Engineering Workbench®, Knowledge Coordinator™, and
KnowledgeWare® are all trademarks of KnowledgeWare, Inc.

IMS, DL/1, and CICS/VSAM are all trade names of IBM
(International Business Machines).

IDMS® is a registered trademark of Cullinet Software, Inc.

CA-DATAMACS® is a registered trademark of Computer
Associates International, Inc.

AY/Computer System Methodology™ is a trademark of
Arthur Young.

Library of Congress Cataloging in Publication Data:

The Arthur Young practical guide to information
  engineering.

  Bibliography: p.
  1. Management information systems.   2. Information
resources management.   I. Arthur Young & Company.

T58.6.A67   1987   658.4'038   87-13320
ISBN 0-471-62920-0

Printed in the United States of America

10 9 8 7 6 5 4 3 2 1

PREFACE

Linking business strategies to systems planning and development strategies has taken on a whole new meaning in today's information-oriented business world. Organizations that proactively seek innovative ways to use information technology to gain a competitive advantage recognize not only the value of but also the need for more formal approaches to accomplish this objective.

More and more, organizations are using Information Engineering principles as a framework for systems planning, design, and development. Three significant factors have contributed to this trend. The first is the focus on "data" rather than the past concentration on "processes" or activities. The second is the evolving technology known as "computer-aided software engineering" or "CASE." The third is the use of graphics concepts that enable top management and users to participate directly in the systems planning, design, and development process.

The keys to successful systems planning and development are integration and experience. Integration applies to three important facets of the evolving systems planning and development process. One is the integration of combined expertise from a broad base of executive talent from the "business" side of the enterprise with the technological expertise of those in the information systems function. Another is the recognition by the information systems organization that "order-of-magnitude increases in productivity" require the integration of policies and practices involving the use of productivity tools, methodologies, project management techniques, quality improvement programs, and training. Finally, an integrated set of case power tools in the hands of skilled and experienced systems builders (using the power of automation for planning, analysis, design, and construction) will deliver higher quality information systems in less time and at a lower cost than ever before.

This book reflects the early, combined experience of Arthur Young International practitioners in the use of the concepts, methods, tools, and techniques of Information Engineering. We want to emphasize that our goal for this Guide is to provide a "first step" in creating a "body of knowledge" on what is clearly an evolving approach to systems building. Arthur Young will continue to document its experience, and we encourage others to join us—each in their own way—in order to enhance the state of the art of systems, planning, design, and development.

INTRODUCTION

The objective of this Guide is to provide a framework for integrating Information Engineering principles into a systems planning and development approach. It discusses the four major phases of the Information Engineering process: Information Systems Planning, Business Area Analysis, System Design, and Construction. In doing so, it presents a collection of diagrams, task descriptions, task outputs, and deliverable outlines.

The concepts and approaches presented here represent "early experience" on what will be a long learning curve. Evolving technology and continuing applications of the principles of Information Engineering will inevitably point to new and different approaches and concepts.

Covered in this volume are the technical aspects of the Information Engineering process. A companion volume addresses the associated management and organizational issues: coordinating multiple, concurrent projects; project management for a single project; team roles and organization; quality assurance; as well as other relevant topics.

The Guide does not present a methodology in the classic sense of the term. Rather, it presents a framework that can be customized for use on a project-by-project basis. Experienced practitioners who already possess the knowledge, skills, and experience of an "Information Engineer" will find this Guide of significant value and use. It is not a manual that provides step-by-step instructions for inexperienced practitioners. Less experienced practitioners, however, will find it an excellent reference for use with other materials and as a supplement to workshop training programs, on-the-job training, and the personal guidance provided by experienced systems professionals.

The Guide's format includes an introductory narrative to establish each phase's context, purpose, and issues for special consideration. Activities are presented as manageable collections of related tasks, with a decomposition diagram to depict these tasks. Tasks are described in a brief narrative that addresses considerations specific to each task. The relationship of task inputs and outputs is illustrated via data flow diagrams. A review of the "Notations" section found in the front of the Guide will aid in reading and interpreting the graphics.

Chapter 1, "Overview of Information Engineering," describes the key characteristics that distinguish Information Engineering from other systems development approaches, and introduces the four phases of Information Engineering.

Chapter 2, "The Role of the Information Engineering Workbench," illustrates the relationship of the Information Engineering Workbench (IEW) tool to both Information Engineering and the methodology described in Chapters 3 through 6.

Chapters 3 through 6 describe the four phases of the Information Engineering life cycle. Each chapter introduces a phase by describing its goals, approach, deliverables, and specific considerations. A phase decomposition diagram is included to depict the activities performed within each phase. Within these chapters, the activities and tasks are presented in logical groups. There is no attempt to prescribe the sequence of actual project team work. In practice, many of the activities and tasks within each phase would be performed either concurrently or iteratively. For many projects, phases may also overlap.

The *"Glossary"* lists Information Engineering terms used within the Guide.

ACKNOWLEDGMENTS

A number of Arthur Young people contributed their time and talent to develop *The Arthur Young Practical Guide to Information Engineering*. They deserve to share any credit for the book's contribution to improving the state of the art of systems planning and development.

We owe special thanks to the following people who provided critical insights from a practitioner's perspective: Dean Bell, Anchorage, Alaska; Mike Burkett, Houston, Texas; Richard Doyle, Arthur Young International, Ann Arbor, Michigan; Suzanne Hain, Reston, Virginia; Jim Harrison, Houston, Texas; Steve Ingram, Sydney, Australia; Al Kortesoja, Ann Arbor, Michigan; Jo Millot, London, United Kingdom; and Kurt Wagner, Seattle, Washington.

Special thanks also go to the New York national office team—not only for their significant contributions to the book's content but also for their skillful handling of all the administrative tasks related to preparing the manuscript. These people include: Yaquelin Abreu, Tom Cordell, Sheryl Daniels, John Denkowski, Frank Ennis, Ed Farrelly, Ruby Holmes, Norma Maldonado, Wendy Moran, Howard Oboler, John Sifonis, George Sorensen, Madeline Velez, and Glen Weekley.

Finally, we thank the thousands of Arthur Young information technology consultants around the world who are continually developing and improving the methods and techniques that translate Information Engineering principles into a practical approach to systems planning and development.

Our close association with James Martin over the past few years has been a significant factor in our interest and ability to publish this Guide. James Martin is recognized as the founder and "champion" of Information Engineering. His critical insights into the vital benefits and values of Information Engineering form the foundation for our work. Through James Martin and his organization, KnowledgeWare, Inc., we have been directly involved in the development of the Information Engineering Workbench. This association provided us with added opportunities as James Martin merged his organization with Tarkenton Software, the originator of GAMMA. Therefore, we acknowledge the significant contributions of James Martin, Fran Tarkenton and the many people in KnowledgeWare, Inc.

CONTENTS

NOTATIONS

The graphics appearing in this Guide use the following symbols:

SYMBOL	MEANING
	Identifies a phase, an activity, or a task on a Decomposition Diagram
→	Identifies a task input or output on a Data Flow Diagram
	Identifies a task on a Data Flow Diagram
	Identifies a phase deliverable on a Data Flow Diagram
	Identifies an intermediate work paper on a Data Flow Diagram

Arthur Young Information Engineering Overview Diagram

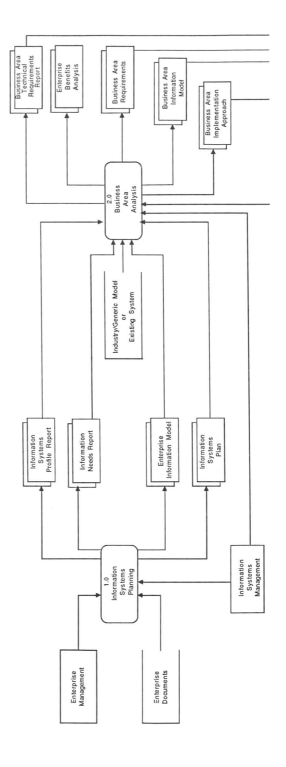

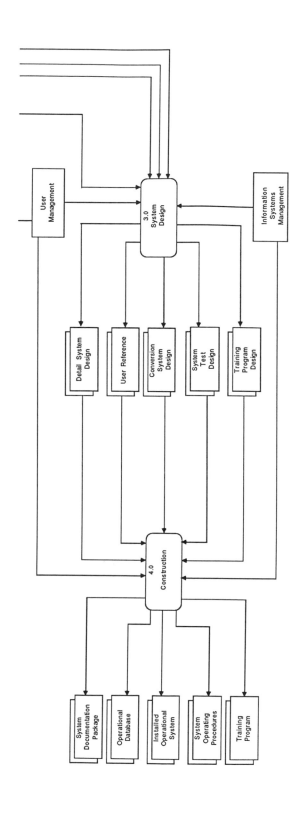

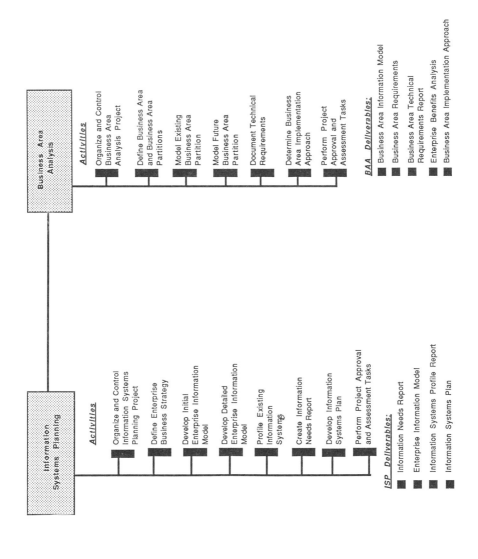

Information Systems Planning

Activities

- Organize and Control Information Systems Planning Project
- Define Enterprise Business Strategy
- Develop Initial Enterprise Information Model
- Develop Detailed Enterprise Information Model
- Profile Existing Information Systems
- Create Information Needs Report
- Develop Information Systems Plan
- Perform Project Approval and Assessment Tasks

ISP Deliverables:

- Information Needs Report
- Enterprise Information Model
- Information Systems Profile Report
- Information Systems Plan

Business Area Analysis

Activities

- Organize and Control Business Area Analysis Project
- Define Business Area and Business Area Partitions
- Model Existing Business Area Partition
- Model Future Business Area Partition
- Document Technical Requirements
- Determine Business Area Implementation Approach
- Perform Project Approval and Assessment Tasks

BAA Deliverables:

- Business Area Information Model
- Business Area Requirements
- Business Area Technical Requirements Report
- Enterprise Benefits Analysis
- Business Area Implementation Approach

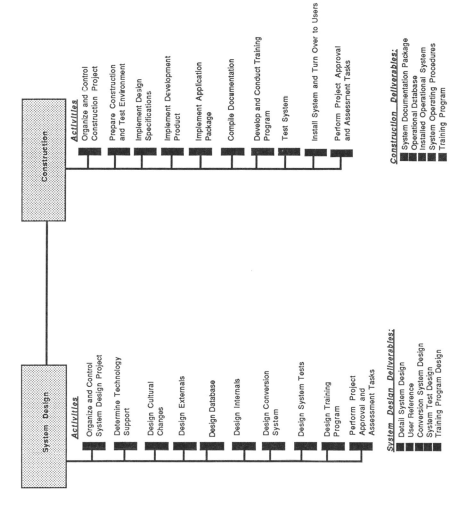

Construction

Activities

- Organize and Control Construction Project
- Prepare Construction and Test Environment
- Implement Design Specifications
- Implement Development Product
- Implement Application Package
- Compile Documentation
- Develop and Conduct Training Program
- Test System
- Install System and Turn Over to Users
- Perform Project Approval and Assessment Tasks

Construction Deliverables:

- System Documentation Package
- Operational Database
- Installed Operational System
- System Operating Procedures
- Training Program

System Design

Activities

- Organize and Control System Design Project
- Determine Technology Support
- Design Cultural Changes
- Design Externals
- Design Database
- Design Internals
- Design Conversion System
- Design System Tests
- Design Training Program
- Perform Project Approval and Assessment Tasks

System Design Deliverables:

- Detail System Design
- User Reference
- Conversion System Design
- System Test Design
- Training Program Design

THE ARTHUR YOUNG
PRACTICAL GUIDE TO
INFORMATION ENGINEERING

1

OVERVIEW OF INFORMATION ENGINEERING

Information Engineering is an approach to planning, defining, designing, and constructing information systems that:

Satisfy enterprise-wide requirements;

Are directly linked to enterprise strategy and goals;

Provide for the most effective and efficient use of information in achieving the enterprise's mission.

Information Engineering uses integrated models or views of the business as the basis for designing and building information systems. This basis ensures that information systems fit the underlying business and provide lasting solutions to enterprise strategy.

The products of Information Engineering are built using an interlocking set of rigorous techniques that maximize product quality and user satisfaction. These techniques are applied using powerful automated tools to increase speed and accuracy and to handle the vast amounts of information required to build information systems.

This chapter describes Information Engineering by examining:

The objectives of Information Engineering;

The key characteristics of Information Engineering;

How Information Engineering differs from traditional information technology approaches;

The advantages of Information Engineering;

The structure of Information Engineering.

THE OBJECTIVES OF INFORMATION ENGINEERING

Support responsively and accurately the information needs of senior managers, primarily through the development of information systems that are of strategic importance to the enterprise.

Focus the efforts of the Information Systems Group by relating information system activities and products to the enterprise goals and Critical Success Factors they support.

Provide senior management with an increased understanding of, and a greater ability to control, the enterprise's information systems resources.

Assist the enterprise in gaining and defending a competitive advantage in the marketplace by identifying strategic uses of information technology.

Decrease the time required to bring new applications into productive use, and reduce the maintenance problems associated with keeping them cost effective and productive.

Involve users more effectively in information systems planning, analysis, and design through the increased use of techniques such as Information Engineering Joint Application Development (IE-JAD) and prototyping.

Improve the quality of information systems software by increasing the rigor of the methods used to create it, and by basing the system design on data and activity models of the underlying business.

THE KEY CHARACTERISTICS OF INFORMATION ENGINEERING

Strong Emphasis on Data Sharing. A tenet of the Information Engineering approach is that data and their inherent structure must be analyzed independently from the applications that may use them, as opposed to functionally oriented approaches that inevitably lead to systems and files biased toward specific business problems, with no guarantee of flexibility or potential integration. Information Engineering uses data models to define business data in a manner that satisfies enterprise-wide data requirements and promotes data sharing. These definitions of data, as represented in the data model, form the foundation for stable databases and system integration.

User-Driven Approach. Information Engineering emphasizes the user role throughout the development process, extending it well into System Design. The driving down of user-supplied Critical Success Factors when designing systems, coupled with an emphasis on techniques such as IE-JAD and prototyping, allow the user to assume a significant role. User access to models (either as developers or as reviewers) is supported by a strong graphics orientation.

Emphasis on Business Analysis. Information Engineering focuses on the front end of the systems building process to a much greater extent than previous approaches. Building logical models of business data and activities (that can be transformed into system designs) provides for an accurate system fit. The concern is to get the planning, analysis, and design correct. If the models are complete and correct, then much of the application code can be generated automatically. To accomplish the timely creation of rigorous models, automated tools are necessary.

Systems Building as an Engineering Discipline. All engineering disciplines are based on formal techniques, and applying formal techniques to the complex, time-sensitive requirements of building information systems is not practical without automated tools. Automated tools impose the formality of an engineering process when they provide for consistency and correctness checking. An additional byproduct of the increased rigor is reduced scope drift, especially during analysis and design efforts. Accurate business-oriented and technical representations of information systems can be built and validated using engineering principles. The representations can in turn be used to construct the final product.

Emphasis on Automation. Design automation linked to code generation offers the potential for extremely high productivity compared with traditional techniques. The use of tools such as the Information Engineering Workbench® (IEW), linked to a comprehensive encyclopedia knowledge base, improves initial planning and accelerates the construction of systems. A critical bridge is the link from design automation, using the IEW, to code generators such as GAMMA™, as well as to more traditional Fourth-Generation Languages. The tools for comput-er-aided system design, when tightly linked to the computerized repre-sentation of the data model, can increase the speed at which systems are built and modified, and most importantly, coordinate the vast amount of knowledge that must be collected and updated to keep information systems supportive of enterprise goals and Critical Success Factors.

Graphics Orientation. Information Engineering attempts to maxi-mize the use of diagrams, which are the primary vehicle for expressing data and activity models. The purpose of the strong graphics orientation is to make communication easier and faster, both among information engineers and between a technical team and users or managers.

Code Generation. Automated code generation is a key strategy of Information Engineering. A rigorous, structured approach to applica-tion development alleviates the enterprise's backlog problem by creat-ing flexible systems requiring less revision and maintenance.

Strategic Foundation. Information Engineering requires a firm, on-going senior management commitment; it is a company-wide activity that needs direction from the top. Information Engineering is tied to management planning through the use of an enterprise's goals and Critical Success Factors. Driving the Critical Success Factor hierarchy down to the system level through Information Engineering ensures that only systems critical to the enterprise are generated. This establishes the ability to trace enterprise strategy to its implementation.

Focus on Developing a Comprehensive Knowledge Base. An enter-prise practicing Information Engineering will need to manipulate sig-nificant amounts of data about itself, including detailed models, orga-nizational and structural details, strategies, and plans. An important objective of Information Engineering is to organize and preserve this information in a knowledge base shared by the entire enterprise. Information Engineering builds a comprehensive knowledge base incre-mentally, permitting an effective integration of applications across the enterprise.

HOW INFORMATION ENGINEERING DIFFERS FROM TRADITIONAL INFORMATION TECHNOLOGY APPROACHES

Information Engineering represents a significant step forward in the development of application software. Although existing structured approaches have sometimes included one or more of the following strategies, Information Engineering supersedes these old ways in that it:

- Channels an Information Systems Group to develop only applications that can be directly linked to the strategic goals, Critical Success Factors and needs of the enterprise;

- Makes extensive use of strongly user-driven tools and techniques, such as Information Engineering Joint Application Development and prototyping, to encourage ongoing participation, which in turn reduces risk and accelerates development;

- Is based on the use of formal data and process models developed via rigorous techniques;

- Is designed to take maximum advantage of automated techniques and tools;

- Emphasizes the use of an enterprise knowledge base (the encyclopedia) that steadily accumulates knowledge about the enterprise and its systems.

THE ADVANTAGES OF INFORMATION ENGINEERING

The systematic use of Information Engineering can provide an enterprise with a number of significant benefits:

- Because Critical Success Factors are used as a steering mechanism for the Information Systems Group, this direct link to an enterprise's strategic goals helps senior management more effectively use information technology as a competitive weapon.

- Information Engineering firmly anchors information technology costs and benefits in senior management planning, where it is expressed in terms of value added to the enterprise.

Information Engineering identifies how to get the right information to the right people at the right time.

The coupling of analysis and design automation to code generation yields very high Information Systems Group productivity.

Information Engineering yields well engineered solutions. The application systems are easy to modify at the model level and can be regenerated, so maintenance problems are greatly reduced.

Information Engineering integrates applications across an enterprise by managing the sources and uses of shared data.

THE STRUCTURE OF INFORMATION ENGINEERING

Information Engineering is an enterprise-wide strategy for creating information systems. The classical Information Engineering metaphor is a three-sided pyramid, as shown in the figure.

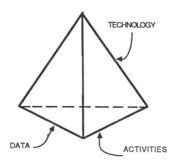

The first side of the pyramid represents data, the second side represents activities, and the third side represents technology. The pyramid illustrates the complex associations among multiple corporate and technological factors that must be identified, planned, integrated, and managed in order for information technology to contribute to enterprise objectives efficiently and effectively.

Another view of the pyramid shows the four phases of Information Engineering.

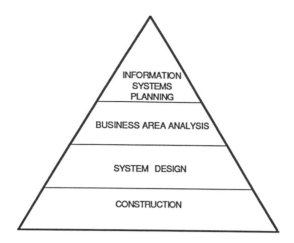

INFORMATION SYSTEMS PLANNING OVERVIEW

Information Systems Planning (ISP) is the initial phase of Information Engineering. During ISP, a high-level model of the enterprise and its data is produced. This model links information requirements to senior management's strategic planning. The business plan used to set targets, goals, and strategies for the enterprise must be reflected in the Information Systems Plan.

Information Systems Planning is valuable to an enterprise because it directs senior management's attention to critical problems and issues both within the enterprise and without. Concise presentations of the planning information—typically diagrams and matrices—foster regular review of goals and Critical Success Factors. The hierarchy of Critical Success Factors often can be tied to the motivation of employees via management by objectives, thereby establishing a mechanism for steering the entire enterprise toward the achievement of its mission.

Goals

Understand and model the enterprise and its use of information from a senior management perspective.

Define Business Areas for the entire enterprise.

Define information infrastructure projects.

Develop tactical and long-range information systems plans.

Document an ongoing planning process.

Approach

Information Systems Planning begins by examining the business plans and strategies of the enterprise. The senior management view of the enterprise is defined and analyzed; and goals, Critical Success Factors, and critical issues are defined and prioritized. An initial and then a more detailed Enterprise Information Model is developed, along with a profile of the existing information systems organizations.

A report that describes the information needs of senior management, functional managers, and the Information Systems Group is created. Based on these needs, a prioritized group of Business Areas is defined. An Information Systems Plan is then developed to define projects over a three- to five-year time frame. The Business Areas are analyzed in Business Area Analysis projects; other infrastructure projects are also carried out.

Considerations

The Information Systems Plan should be understandable to senior management, information systems management, and line management. It should be reviewed and updated as part of the enterprise's business planning cycle.

A well prepared Information Systems Plan will enable the enterprise to make informed decisions in six areas:

Information needs of senior executives and line managers;

Priority areas for new or enhanced application systems to support the business;

Technology strategies that should be employed;

Organizational issues, including the mission and charter of the Information Systems Group;

The management practices needed to better manage information technology resources; and

The migration approach to develop the enterprise's current use of information technology to the desired state.

The use of the Information Engineering Workbench (IEW) allows the planning information to serve as the foundation for Business Area Analysis.

BUSINESS AREA ANALYSIS OVERVIEW

The Business Area Analysis (BAA) phase follows the Information Systems Planning (ISP) phase where enterprise strategy was studied to identify and set the boundaries for a focused BAA project. The purpose of BAA is to create a logical information model that reflects the interrelationships of data, activities, and enterprise goals associated with the Business Area. This logical view, called the Business Area Information Model, becomes the basis for defining system design concepts that fit the underlying business and support its goals. The model provides an architecture for designing integrated information systems across the Business Area.

Goals

Accurately model the Business Area, developing detailed data and activity models; and document the models using Information Engineering methods, techniques, and tools.

Determine which Business Area activities are most important in defining enterprise goals and Critical Success Factors.

Using the model as a framework, identify potential system design alternatives.

Determine design and implementation priorities by mapping the costs and benefits for each project onto the goals and Critical Success Factors associated with the Business Area.

Approach

The ISP deliverables are reviewed to verify the understanding of enterprise strategy and BAA scope. Once the Business Area project definition is accepted, analysis commences and the Business Area model is constructed. Business Area activities and data are decomposed, and detailed data content, data flows, and business policy are defined. The result is a Business Area Information Model. After the logical model is completed, the current Business Area environment is assessed, and potential design concepts are nominated using the model. Finally, design concepts are prioritized via enterprise benefit analysis; and an implementation approach is selected.

Considerations

The phase prior to BAA, ISP, is dedicated to defining and documenting enterprise strategic directions and to ensuring that the focus of the BAA project addresses enterprise needs. If ISP has not been performed, a scaled-down version of ISP should be executed to develop a rough-cut enterprise model. The second activity of the BAA phase, "Define Business Area and Business Area Partitions," should produce a sufficient model.

When modeling a Business Area, analysis must be undertaken independently of technology considerations and of the mechanisms currently used to implement systems. To encourage this approach, the analysis tasks in the methodology are organized to separate the study of logical business operations and information from their physical execution and implementation. Logical modeling is done first, followed by the consideration of physical and technical constraints.

Data and activity analyses are normally completed in parallel as complementary tasks, each providing the other with better insight into the Business Area. To ensure that they correspond, data and activity model fragments should be consolidated. This leads to the completion of correct models.

SYSTEM DESIGN OVERVIEW

System Design is the third phase of Information Engineering. During System Design, Information Engineers transform the requirements reveled by BAA into detailed application system specifications. Users should be deeply involved in the design process. This level of involvement can be achieved in a variety of ways, including:

Allowing users to design system-related manual procedures—ideally, using the IEW;

Prototyping, particularly for user (nonautomated) interfaces;
Conducting IE-JAD sessions.

Goals

Ensure that the design supports the goals and Critical Success Factors associated with the relevant Business Area.

Verify that the design will satisfy user requirements, while giving the user a strong influence over the external design by using prototypes as a communication vehicle.

Enhance project quality and communication between project team members by using standard models and well documented work steps.

Plan system conversion, user training, testing and acceptance procedures, and the implementation strategy.

Approach

A framework for design is created by determining the overall technological support required for the project and any cultural changes necessary to support the new system. The design of externals and of the database precedes and sets the target for internal design. Prototyping is a frequently used design technique because it facilitates communication with users and provides a phased implementation approach.

The conversion system; system test plans, scripts and acceptance criteria; and user and operator training programs are designed to complete this phase.

Considerations

The use of the IEW and GAMMA will have a significant impact on the design effort. Not only will design work be accelerated, but the designer can continually edit the design, each time enhancing detail. The IEW assists by providing details about data and activities, and by verifying the design through integrity checks. The designer must create a well structured design, and the IEW enforces this. The IEW also requires designs that provide a basis for full or partial code generation.

Similarly, the use of GAMMA's Design Manual is a powerful way to organize and manage System Design phase deliverables.

The Construction and System Design phases will often proceed in parallel. For example, after a subsystem is designed, it can be constructed while other subsystems are being designed. Prototypes can be turned over to construction on a subsystem-by-subsystem basis. Also, the conversion software often can be developed and tested during design of the application.

CONSTRUCTION OVERVIEW

Construction is the fourth phase of the Information Engineering process. In Construction, the organization implements the system solutions defined in the System Design phase. Since the designs have been developed with rigorous, engineering-like methods, large portions of the system can be generated by employing a code generator, such as GAMMA or a Fourth-Generation Language. During this phase, the organization also develops procedures for operating the system and trains users to use the system effectively.

Goals

Construct and install a high quality system which conforms to the design specifications.

Meet the guidelines of the enterprise for system auditability, security, and data archiving.

Develop procedures for the day-to-day operation and maintenance of the system.

Provide a training program and conduct the training.

Approach

Two types of specification may be implemented:

Specifications for implementing a development product from an internal design specification;

Specifications for implementing selected application packages.

Support activities needed regardless of the approach selected include training, system testing, production of final system documentation, and installation of the system in its production environment.

Considerations

An emphasis on analysis and design efforts means that Construction begins with detailed, accurate specifications that can be used to generate the application code.

Portions of Construction may overlap BAA or System Design. For example, the building of prototypes, the conversion of data, and the preparation of the Construction and test environment often occur early in the development cycle.

2

THE ROLE OF THE INFORMATION ENGINEERING WORKBENCH

Automated tools are critical to both Information Engineering and methodologies employing its techniques. Not only are there productivity gains associated with the use of tools, but the introduction of tools also changes the fundamental quality of the nature of work, affecting where and when it is done, and what is thought about and managed. An Information Engineering methodology, while prescriptive in its tool recommendations, is not bound by them. It is clear, however, that the most powerful way to implement Information Engineering is by using a tool set such as the Information Engineering Workbench (IEW). Conversely, to provide the needed rigor and to acquire the full benefit of power tools, it is necessary to depend on Information Engineering.

The IEW is an integrated collection of tools that share a knowledge base (the Encyclopedia). Information collected early in the Information Engineering process becomes easily available as analysts and implementors progress to the more detailed stages.

To be fully effective, an Information Engineering methodology must be supported by both modeling tools and a code generator, which allow automation of the system design process and the involvement of users in design and prototyping. An Information Engineering methodology links these important approaches with system building tools.

This chapter looks at the Information Engineering Workbench as it relates to the methodology and maps IEW tool recommendations against the methodology.

INFORMATION ENGINEERING WORKBENCH OVERVIEW

This brief description focuses on:

The Encyclopedia
Information Engineering Workbench tools
Workstation features.

The Encyclopedia

The IEW Encyclopedia is a central repository of knowledge about the enterprise and its goals, structure, functions, processes, procedures, and programs. Data models and activity models are stored in the Encyclopedia, as well as facts about and policies governing the enterprise and its systems. The Encyclopedia is built up, one project at a time, as the enterprise practices Information Engineering.

The Encyclopedia is a knowledge base that stores many different types of data and rules relating to the data. The Encyclopedia uses several artificial intelligence techniques to ensure that all requisite information is gathered and cross-coordinated.

Information Engineering Workbench Tools

Knowledge is communicated to the Encyclopedia via diagrams. Diagrams are essential to the practice of Information Engineering and are to be used whenever possible as an aid to clear thinking.

Information Engineering depends on a complete, integrated, rigorous set of diagramming standards. The diagrams must be complete enough and rigorous enough to serve as a basis for code generation and for automatic conversion of one type of diagram into another. To ensure rigor, the IEW uses a Knowledge Coordinator™, a complex encyclopedia manager employing hundreds of logic rules to enforce standards and automatically validate models. To support the need for complete and correct diagrams, a set of diagramming tools is included in the IEW:

Decomposition Diagrammer®
Entity Diagrammer®
Data Flow Diagrammer™
Action Diagrammer®.

Decomposition Diagrammer. This tool allows for the creation and maintenance of hierarchy diagrams for Subject Areas, activities, and organizational units. The Decomposition Diagrammer automatically enforces the rules of decomposition, alerting the user to circular relationships among objects. Decomposition Diagrammer is used extensively during the Information Systems Planning and Business Area Analysis phases of Information Engineering.

Entity Diagrammer. This tool allows the user to diagram the entity types of concern to the enterprise, and helps determine the relationships among them. Both minimum and maximum cardinalities can be specified to distinguish optional relationships from mandatory ones. Entity Diagrammer can use information implied by individual entity diagrams for specific activities, data flows, and data stores to automatically construct an entity diagram for the integrated entity model. This tool is used during Information Systems Planning, Business Area Analysis, and System Design.

Data Flow Diagrammer. With this tool, the user can diagram activities, along with the data stores, junctions, external agents, and data flows that are associated with an activity. Data flow expressions are used to describe data flow contents. A leveled set of data flow diagrams can be generated automatically, one for each object on a decomposition diagram. Each generated diagram is populated with symbols for the subactivities of the node in the decomposition diagram. This tool is most closely associated with Business Area Analysis.

Action Diagrammer. This tool uses both graphic and narrative notation to represent hierarchical structure, repetition, case structure, exits, database actions, and common subprocedures. Brackets are the basic building blocks of action diagrams. Nesting of multiple brackets shows the process (and subprocess) hierarchy triggered by execution decisions and conditions. The Encyclopedia stores all action diagram logic details, providing the level of detail needed to support code generation. Action Diagrammer is used within Business Area Analysis, System Design, and Construction.

GAMMA. An application generator that interfaces with the IEW, GAMMA is an interactive tool that supports Information Engineering during the System Design and Construction phases. A GAMMA feature called the Design Manual helps organize and manage the design specifications that will drive the automatic generation of code. GAMMA provides a COBOL-like syntax for the manual creation of custom procedural logic, and supports major database management systems, including IMS/DC, DL/1, CICS/VSAM and IDMS.

Workstation Features of the Information Engineering Workbench

The magnitude of the diagrammatic requirements of Information Engineering makes the automated tools of the IEW essential. Diagrams are built and displayed on a workstation screen. The workstation interacts with analysts, planners, designers, and users to provide computer-aided design. Through zooming, windowing, nesting, and other graphic management techniques, the workstation can handle diagrams that would be excessively complex if drawn on paper.

The mouse-driven IEW provides the ability to view several diagrams at once through multiple windows. This allows the user to track more easily the flow of data or the sequence of operations through several diagrams.

Tool Recommendations

Appropriate IEW tool use is expressed by the following diagram:

Information Engineering Workbench Tools	Information Engineering Phases			
	Information Systems Planning	Business Area Analysis	System Design	Construction
Entity Diagrammer	x	x	x	
Decomposition Diagrammer	x	x	x	
Data Flow Diagrammer		x		
Action Diagrammer		x	x	x
GAMMA Code Generator			x	x

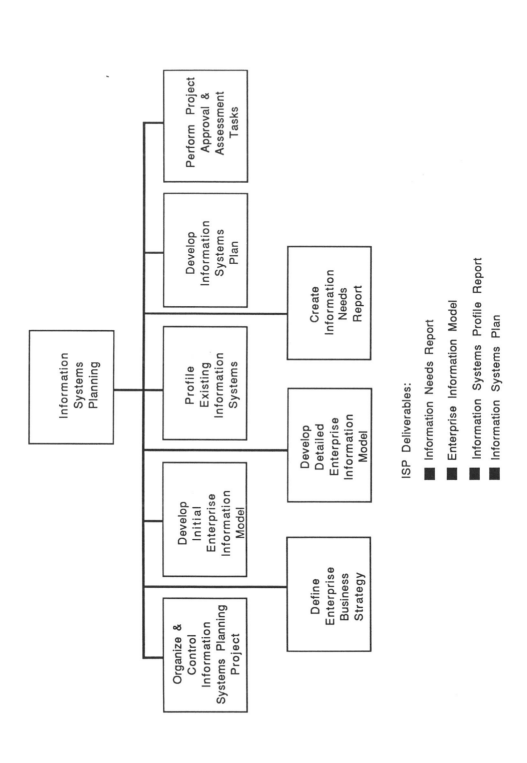

Information Systems Planning

- Organize & Control Information Systems Planning Project
- Develop Initial Enterprise Information Model
  - Define Enterprise Business Strategy
- Profile Existing Information Systems
  - Develop Detailed Enterprise Information Model
- Develop Information Systems Plan
  - Create Information Needs Report
- Perform Project Approval & Assessment Tasks

ISP Deliverables:

- ■ Information Needs Report
- ■ Enterprise Information Model
- ■ Information Systems Profile Report
- ■ Information Systems Plan

3

INFORMATION SYSTEMS PLANNING PHASE

Information Systems Planning (ISP) is the initial phase of the Information Engineering process. During ISP, an enterprise decides what information systems and services are needed, what resources are required to provide these systems and services, and how the information systems function should be managed.

Information Systems Planning enables an enterprise to make decisions in six areas:

Information needs: the identification of information needs of senior executives and functional (line) managers, as well as descriptions of data that can satisfy these needs.

Applications: the identification of priority areas for new or enhanced application systems to support the business, and the preparation of a high-level project plan to develop and effect solutions.

Technology strategies and resources: the identification of appropriate technologies, and the amount and types of resources needed.

Organization: how resources should be grouped and the mission and charter of each group in the overall information systems function.

Management practices: identifying their underlying principles, and using them to manage the information systems resources.

Migration: how to move the organization's use of information systems from its present state to the desired state.

Goals

View the enterprise and its use of information from a senior management perspective.

Construct an Enterprise Information Model to document this understanding.

Define information technology-related projects for the enterprise.

Develop an Information Systems Plan that defines projects over a three- to five-year period.

Document an ongoing planning process.

Approach

Information Systems Planning begins with an examination of the business plans and strategies of the enterprise. The senior management view of the enterprise is defined and analyzed; and goals, Critical Success Factors, and other critical issues are uncovered and prioritized. An initial and then a more detailed Enterprise Information Model is developed, along with a profile of the existing information systems organization.

A report is written, describing the information needs of senior management, functional managers, and the Information Systems Group. Based on these needs, Business Areas are grouped according to priority. An Information Systems Plan then defines projects to be completed over the next three to five years. The Business Areas are analyzed in Business Area Analysis projects; other infrastructure projects are also completed.

Deliverables

Information Needs Report
Enterprise Information Model
Information Systems Profile Report
Information Systems Plan

Considerations

An Information Systems Plan is most useful, and is more likely to add significant value, when developed by a combined team of senior and line managers and Information Systems Group personnel. An ISP team that draws upon multiple perspectives and varied experiences within the enterprise (perhaps supplemented by external consultants with firsthand, current industry knowledge) is well positioned to create a useful information systems baseline.

ORGANIZE AND CONTROL INFORMATION SYSTEMS PLANNING PROJECT

The management tasks identified for this phase reflect the general activities and responsibilities of project management. To initiate and manage the project, perform the following tasks:

Organize and train the project team;

Develop and revise the work unit plan;

Review actual versus planned activities;

Review work products;

Analyze the consistency of project definitions and the proposed design;

Evaluate change requests;

Review and revise control procedures;

Report on project status;

Perform short-interval scheduling.

DEFINE ENTERPRISE BUSINESS STRATEGY

The purpose of this activity is to determine and document the goals and Critical Success Factors by which an enterprise measures its success. A prioritized set of goals and Critical Success Factors, consolidated to reflect the collected vision of senior management, is used to drive the ISP process. Typically, a formal executive interviewing process is used to obtain a current set of goals and Critical Success Factors that are fully supported by the existing senior management team, and that are also fully consistent and supportive of the enterprise's current business plans and strategies. In addition, the technology plans that exist are evaluated; and senior management information needs are documented.

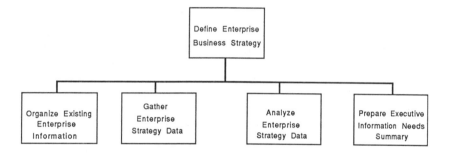

Organize Existing Enterprise Information

In this task, the objective is to collect the existing documents that will form the baseline for conducting the study and to evaluate their usefulness for the project. As orientation aids, these documents can help the project team to understand the structure of the enterprise and to identify strategies already established. This task provides the basis for determining the work that must be carried out in ISP.

To accomplish this task, compile existing documents, including:

Business plans;

Proposal/Charter for the ISP study;

Information Technology Plans;

Other sources of information, such as:

      Critical Success Factor studies,

      Annual reports,

Data models,

System architecture documents,

Organization and staffing charts,

Job descriptions.

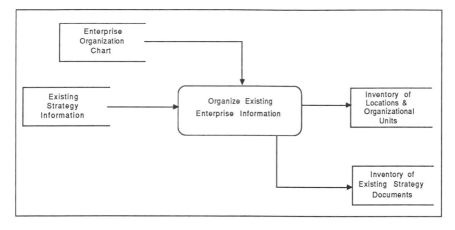

Evaluate the condition and usefulness of the collected documents, and inventory the enterprise's major locations and organizational units. Study (or develop, if necessary) a current organization chart and associate enterprise locations with organizational units.

Gather Enterprise Strategy Data

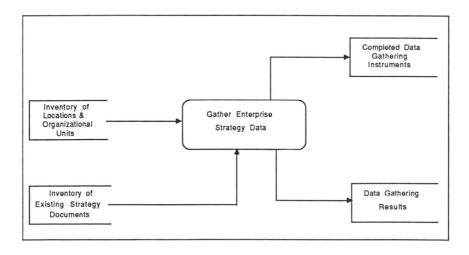

Current strategic enterprise information is gathered by conducting senior management interviews and analyzing collected documents. Based on an evaluation of the documents collected, determine sources for missing strategic information and determine the best source for obtaining it (e.g., from senior management, line management, or existing documents such as strategic plans). Develop data-gathering instruments, such as questionnaires and forms, to aid the collection of missing information from appropriate sources.

Conduct data-gathering activities (such as interviews and document reviews) and compile the collected information, which includes, but is not limited to:

Critical Success Factors

Goals and problems

Critical information needs

Critical assumptions

Critical decisions

Technology issues.

Analyze Enterprise Strategy Data

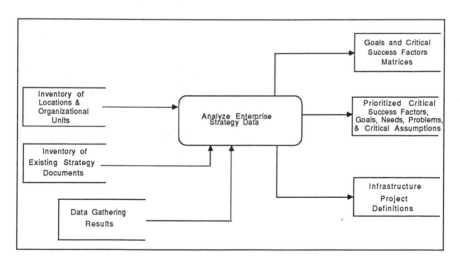

The purpose of this task is to refine and validate the collected information and to identify relationships among significant enterprise data. Collected information is also prioritized according to strategic significance. In addition, critical or high-visibility infrastructure projects that can be initiated without waiting for ISP completion are defined so they can be set in motion. Such projects would include those not oriented to any specific business application, such as establishing a Database Administrator function or conducting Business Area Analysis training.

Identify and categorize (as direct, indirect or through a numeric weighing schema) the following matrix relationships:

Critical Success Factors versus goals;

Critical Success Factors versus critical information needs.

If appropriate, analyze additional relationships, such as Critical Success Factors to locations or organizational units. Rank Critical Success Factors, goals, critical assumptions, problems, and needs based on their conformance to enterprise mission; their impact on Critical Success Factors, goals, and critical assumptions by problems and needs; the frequency with which they are mentioned during the interviews, and by whom; and the importance attached by senior management. Review the collected information needs, looking for cases where a need can be met quickly by an infrastructure project (e.g., through better use of an existing information center) without full application development. Define the infrastructure projects. Infrastructure projects should be spun off immediately if they are determined to be critical to the enterprise. (Examples of critical infrastructure projects are strategic system opportunities and decision systems that support Critical Success Factors.)

Prepare Executive Information Needs Summary

The objective of this task is to produce a summary of the information and technology requirements of the enterprise from a senior management perspective. To accomplish this objective, study the strategic information collected in the previous tasks of this activity, including the matrices covering goals and Critical Success Factors, and analyze the data. Identify as strategic information needs those situations where information technology affects enterprise systems.

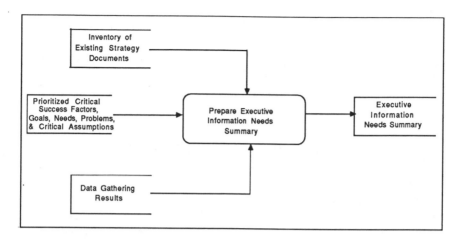

Identify high-level technology choices made by the enterprise as strategic technology directions (such as commitment to a specific hardware environment or communications network). Finally, consolidate findings and conclusions concerning information needs, and prepare the Information Needs Summary.

DEVELOP INITIAL ENTERPRISE INFORMATION MODEL

This activity is performed to develop a high-level model of the data used by the enterprise (an entity-relationship model), as well as Subject Area and Business Function decompositions of the enterprise.

The Enterprise Information Model is cross-referenced with enterprise goals and Critical Success Factors to determine how the model addresses strategic parameters. The output of this activity may satisfy the modeling requirements of Information Systems Planning, depending on the level of detail desired.

Interviews with functional managers are called for in several tasks, both in this activity and in the next. In practice, a manager will typically be interviewed in depth once; and information concerning the manager's knowledge of activities and data (as well as any information needs) will be collected in appropriate detail. (At this point, it is generally known whether a complete Enterprise Information Model, extended to the process and entity-type level, is to be created, or if an abbreviated model will be sufficient.) Of course, follow-up interviews—either with the same manager or with a colleague—are a critical validation step.

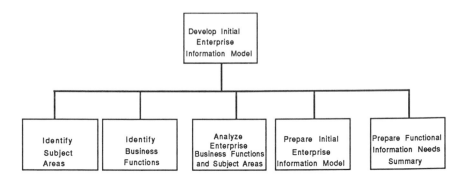

Identify Subject Areas

The purpose of this task is to identify the Subject Areas that comprise the major high-level classifications for the data maintained by the enterprise. To accomplish this task, interview enterprise functional (line) managers and build a decomposition diagram to show the hierar-

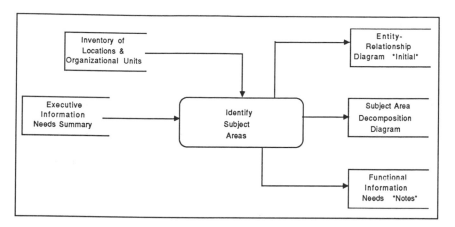

chy of Subject Areas. Decompose Subject Areas two levels down, with each level having from three to seven objects. Finally, identify and document the functional information needs that surface during interviews with line managers and during the decomposition process.

Identify Business Functions

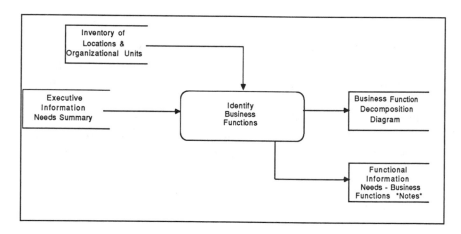

In this task, identify the Business Functions that comprise the major high-level activities the enterprise requires to satisfy its information needs. Interview enterprise functional (line) managers. Decompose Business Functions two levels down, with each decomposition having from three to seven objects. Identify functional information needs that surface during interviews with line managers and during the decomposition process.

Analyze Enterprise Business Functions and Subject Areas

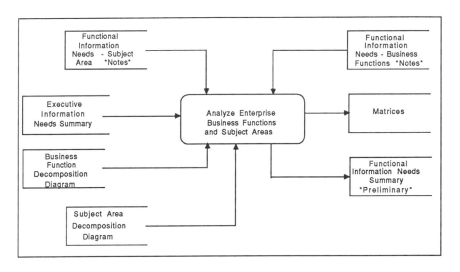

To understand how information supports the enterprise, analyze enterprise Business Functions and Subject Areas. Determine where and by whom the information is used. Next, refine and validate the Subject Area and Business Function decompositions.

Study the following relationships to gain a deeper understanding of the enterprise: (If the Enterprise Information Model is to be driven down to the process/entity-type level, it may not be worth the investment to create associations at this level; instead, the team should wait until it is time to perform the lower-level Subject Area and Business Function analysis.)

Critical Success Factors versus Subject Areas;

Business Functions versus Critical Success Factors.

Identify functional information needs that surface during this analysis, and consolidate into a summary the needs identified thus far.

Prepare Initial Enterprise Information Model

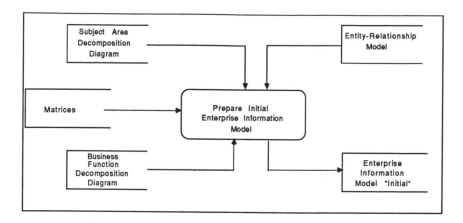

The purpose of this task is to consolidate and document the enterprise information (i.e., Subject Areas, Business Functions, and relationships) into an integrated model. This model will serve as a presentation and communication vehicle and will be extended, if necessary, to provide logically cohesive Business Area definitions.

To accomplish this, document or verify the relevant decompositions and relationships, using decomposition diagrams and entity-relationship diagrams. Verify that Subject Area and Business Function decompositions and relationships are complete and consistent with known enterprise information, and revise them as required.

Prepare Functional Information Needs Summary

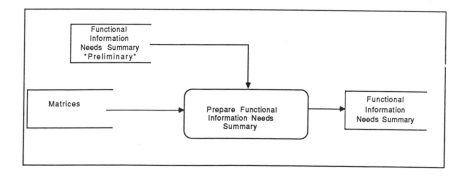

The purpose of this task is to produce a summary of the information and technology requirements of the enterprise from the perspective of operational and functional management. This may be a draft document that is passed along to the activity "Develop Detailed Enterprise Information Model," if a more refined model is required. Analyze functional management interview notes and related information needs documents to determine needs, and then consolidate the findings and conclusions in a report.

DEVELOP DETAILED ENTERPRISE INFORMATION MODEL

The purpose of this activity is to refine and extend the initial Enterprise Information Model. It follows the same sequence as the initial modeling activity, but extends the model. This activity may be bypassed if the existing model is sufficient to guide the development of tactical and long-range information systems plans. More important, the Enterprise Information Model must provide sufficient detail to allow the definition of logical, cohesive Business Areas. Interviews should be conducted as a verification check for model completeness and accuracy and to ensure user ownership of the model.

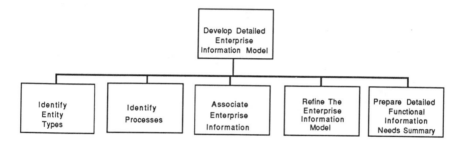

Identify Entity Types

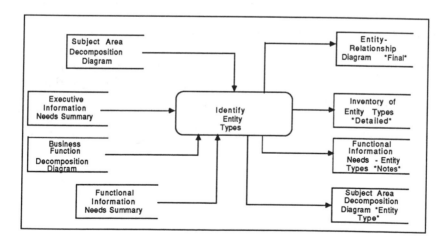

By further decomposing Subject Areas, identify the set of entity types that the enterprise maintains. To complete this task, interview functional (line) representatives to help identify the entity types for each Subject Area. Use decomposition diagrams to decompose the Subject Areas to a third level. Create from three to seven objects for each second level object. Document the relationships between entity types. Verify these with functional (line) representatives using the entity-relationship diagram. As informational needs surface, add them to the list of functional information needs.

Identify Processes

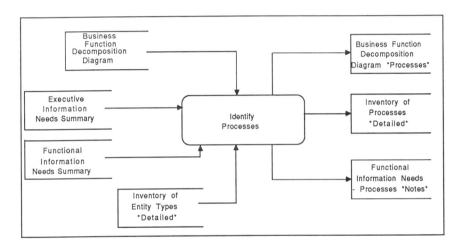

Identify the processes required to satisfy the information needs of the enterprise by further decomposing Business Functions. Matrixed to entity types, processes are a critical input for defining Business Areas. Interview functional (line) representatives to identify the processes comprising each Business Function. Decompose the Business Functions to a third level, creating from three to seven objects for each second-level object. As needs surface, add to the list of functional information needs.

Associate Enterprise Information

The purpose of this task is to validate the completeness and consistency of the entity type and process decompositions. To accomplish this, analyze the meaningful associations among collected information.

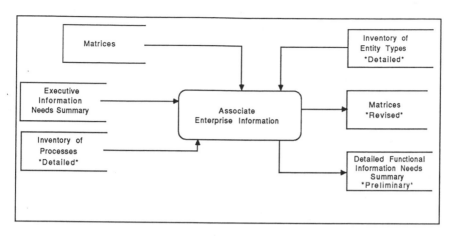

Refine the Enterprise Information Model

This task is performed to refine the existing Enterprise Information Model. Refine, if necessary, the Subject Area and Business Function decompositions in accordance with the more precise entity type and process decompositions. Also refine, if necessary, the entity-relationship diagram in accordance with the more precise entity type and process decompositions.

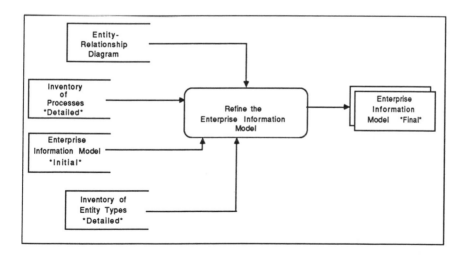

Prepare Detailed Functional Information Needs Summary

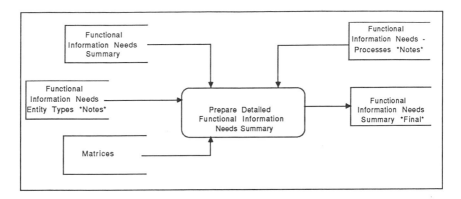

A detailed Information Needs Summary is prepared by producing a summary of the information and technology requirements of the enterprise from a line management perspective. To accomplish this, consolidate information needs by studying interview notes and preliminary Functional Information Needs Summary drafts. Prepare and finalize a draft document after analyzing the needs and consolidating the findings and conclusions.

PROFILE EXISTING INFORMATION SYSTEMS

This activity is carried out to evaluate the information technology capability the enterprise currently has in place. The current application development and maintenance portfolio is examined, and existing data files and processing methods are evaluated in terms of their efficiency and effectiveness. Systems are mapped to the goals and Critical Success Factors of the enterprise. If appropriate, other components of an enterprise's information technology capability are also evaluated. Examples include:

An information center;

Telecommunications (voice and data);

The use of enabling advanced technology (expert, decision support, or executive support systems);

End-user computing;

Hardware acquisition and use;

Office Automation Systems;

Technology planning and control functions.

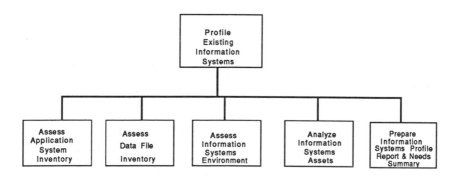

Assess Application System Inventory

The purpose of this task is to identify and assess the effectiveness of methods by which enterprise processes are currently executed. These systems may be automated, manual, or a combination of the two.

Through the data-gathering methods of interviewing and document gathering, identify all application systems. Develop a meaning-

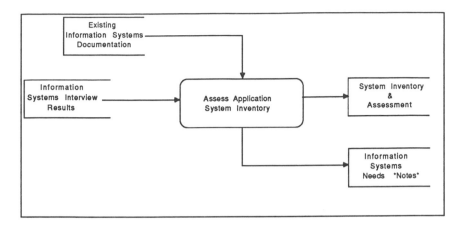

ful method for evaluating current application systems, and assess them using the determined criteria.

Assess Data File Inventory

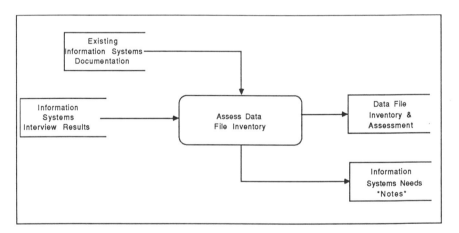

The purpose of this task is to identify the automated or manual files that contain information used by the enterprise, and to assess how useful and appropriate they are. This is completed through data-gathering methods such as interviewing and document gathering. Using these methods, identify all enterprise data files and assess the usefulness, accessibility, reliability, and availability of these files.

Assess Information Systems Environment

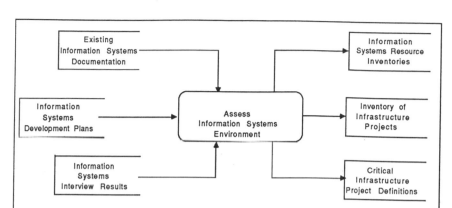

This task is performed to determine the effectiveness and appropriateness of the information technology and resources currently being used by the enterprise.

Inventory the application-independent components of the information systems environment, such as hardware, systems software, voice and data communications, office systems, end-user computing, quality assurance, training, production and distribution services, enabling technologies (such as expert systems and computer-aided software engineering), and the Information Systems Group organization and personnel. Also inventory current plans for the information systems environment and for the development of applications.

With respect to an industry baseline and good management practices, evaluate the information systems environment and plan. Identify projects to address any discovered weaknesses in the information systems environment. If these are critical or prerequisite to application projects, define and initiate them as infrastructure projects. Otherwise, they will be reviewed in the "Synthesize Information Needs" task and formally defined in the "Define Infrastructure Projects" task.

Analyze Information Systems Assets

The purpose of this task is to document and analyze the relationships among existing information systems assets. Based on situational needs, use the following matrices:

Systems versus processes;

Systems versus Critical Success Factors.

Analyze the significance of discrepancies between the existing application portfolio and Critical Success Factor and goal coverage requirements.

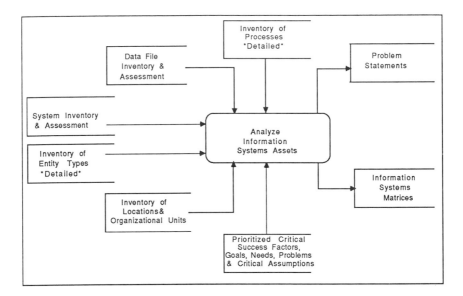

Prepare Information Systems Profile Report and Needs Summary

The purpose of this task is to finalize the results of the information systems organization study. To prepare the reports, review and refine the Information Systems Profile Report, and consolidate and document the Information Systems Needs Summary.

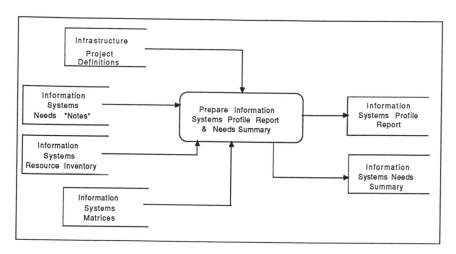

CREATE INFORMATION NEEDS REPORT

This activity consolidates all the collected information needs and produces a formal report. This involves integrating the needs that surfaced during interviews with representatives of executive management, functional (line) operations, and the information systems organization.

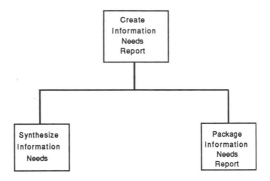

Synthesize Information Needs

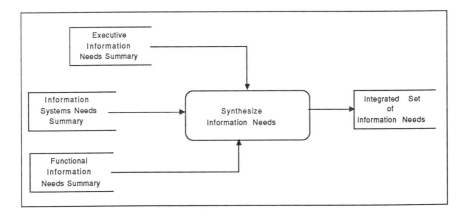

The purpose of this task is to consolidate and document the significant information needs of the enterprise into an approved set. To do this, analyze all needs summaries and resolve inconsistencies, conflicts, and redundancies. Identify and reconcile functional and executive needs.

Identify infrastructure projects by indicating where they are required (e.g., Decision Support Systems to satisfy a particular need, or the cre-

ation of a Database Administrator function). Review the projects identified in the "Analyze Enterprise Strategy Data" task and in the "Assess
Information Systems Environment" task. Spin off projects immediately if they are critical to the enterprise. Review the consolidated
list in meetings with executives, functional representatives, and information systems representatives to refine the integrated list of needs.
Preliminary approvals may be received in these meetings.

Package Information Needs Report

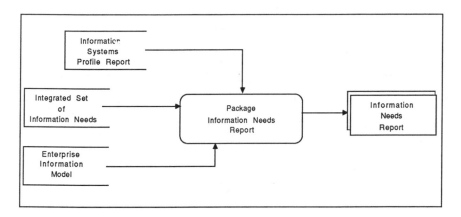

This task is used to package a report summarizing the information needs
of the enterprise. To do so, gather the information needs documents,
revising them as required.

DEVELOP INFORMATION SYSTEMS PLAN

The objective of this activity is to document formally the recommendations of the Information Systems Planning phase. Business Areas are defined for future Business Area Analysis studies. In addition, infrastructure support projects are defined. All projects are prioritized and included on either the tactical or long-range project schedules. Finally, an ongoing planning review and maintenance process is developed.

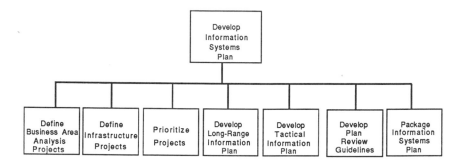

Define Business Area Analysis Projects

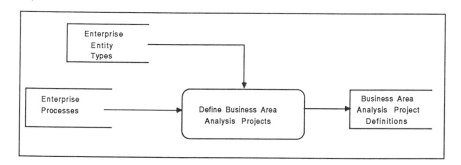

This task's objective is to partition the enterprise into well defined, logically cohesive Business Areas that can be studied meaningfully as independent Business Area Analysis projects. This is accomplished by delineating candidate BAA project boundaries and identifying the initial sets of entity types and processes to be included in each BAA project. Cluster entity types and processes based on their common associations with other ISP data (such as critical problems or Critical Success

Factors). Cluster using affinity analysis, activity life-cycle analysis, and/or factor analysis. Each cluster of entity types and associated activities defines a Business Area project.

Modify the clusters of entity types according to the access type, with activities that *create* entities having the strongest bond, activities that *delete* entities having the next strongest bond, activities that *update* entities having the third strongest, and activities that *read* entities having the weakest bond. Associate processes with BAA projects.

Refine candidate BAA project boundaries according to practical considerations such as Critical Success Factors, cost versus benefits, the current information systems environment, risk, and resources. The adjusted groupings define BAA projects.

Define Infrastructure Projects

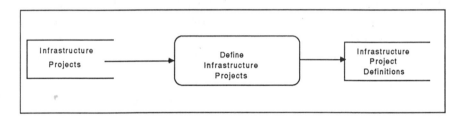

The purpose of this task is to define projects previously identified in the Information Systems Plan that are not specific to a particular Business Area, but are needed to support the overall technology strategies of the enterprise. To do so, pinpoint infrastructure projects that were identified previously but have not yet been spun off as critical projects. (Such infrastructure projects were defined in the "Analyze Enterprise Strategy Data" task and in the "Synthesize Information Needs" task.)

Prioritize Projects

Rank all candidate BAA and infrastructure projects that have been defined for the enterprise. Develop an approach for prioritizing the defined projects. For example, projects may be ranked in order of the extent to which they are directly related to Critical Success Factors (CSFs), with the project showing the most direct links ranked first. Approaches for ranking projects can range from simple measurements

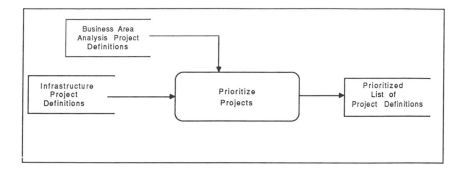

(such as cost or size) to very sophisticated weighting systems. Critical Success Factor ranking is the preferred method.

Develop Long-Range Information Plan

Develop a two- to five-year plan for allocating future information systems resources. Determine the lower priority BAA and infrastructure projects. Schedule the BAA and infrastructure projects over a two- to five-year time horizon and develop a short description for each project.

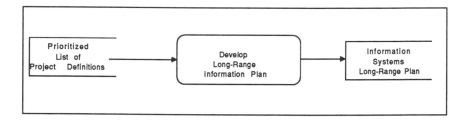

Develop Tactical Information Plan

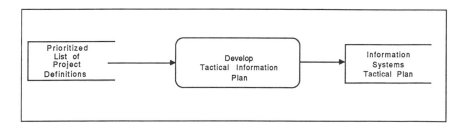

The objective of this task is to create a 12- to 24-month plan for information systems projects. To accomplish this, develop concise and complete project definition descriptions for each scheduled project. Estimate the resource requirements for the highest priority BAA and infrastructure projects. Schedule the highest priority BAA and infrastructure projects for the next one to two years, consistent with available budgets and resources.

Develop Plan Review Guidelines

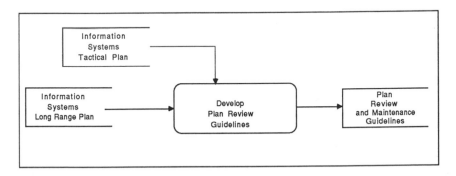

To maintain the Information Systems Plan, develop plan review and maintenance guidelines. Establish policies and procedures for reviewing and updating the plan regularly. Determine the responsibilities and authorities of the involved organizational units, and coordinate the information system review cycle with the enterprise business planning cycle.

Package Information Systems Plan

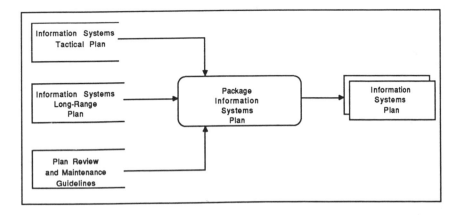

The purpose of this task is to organize for formal review and approval the documents that comprise the Information Systems Plan. Assemble the information systems tactical plan, the information systems long-range plan, and the plan review and maintenance guidelines. Publish and distribute the final Information Systems Plan. Review these documents with enterprise management, and revise them as required.

PERFORM PROJECT APPROVAL AND ASSESSMENT TASKS

The final activity of the ISP phase is to perform the approval and assessment tasks required to complete an ISP project. To accomplish this, obtain approvals and sign-offs for phase deliverables and assess the performance of team members. Reconcile "actuals versus planned" for task results, and perform variance analysis.

INFORMATION SYSTEMS PLANNING DELIVERABLE OUTLINE

I. Information Needs Report
   A. Executive Information Needs Summary
      Strategic Information Needs
      Strategic Technology Directions
   B. Functional Information Needs Summary
   C. Detailed Functional Information Needs Summary
   D. Information Systems Needs Summary
II. Enterprise Information Model
   A. Functional Decomposition—three levels
   B. Entity-Relationship Diagram
   C. Inventories
      Organization
      Locations
      Subject Areas
      Entity Types
      Business Functions
      Processes
   D. Decomposition Diagrams
      Organization
      Subject Areas
      Subject Areas and Entity Types
      Business Functions
      Business Functions and Processes
   E. Matrices (as appropriate)
      Critical Success Factors versus Goals
      Critical Success Factors versus Critical Information Needs
      Critical Success Factors versus Business Functions
      Entity Types versus Processes
      Application Systems versus Processes
      Application Systems versus Critical Success Factors
III. Information Systems Profile Report
   A. Application System Inventory and Assessment
   B. Data File Inventory and Assessment
   C. Application-Independent Component Inventory and Assessment

    D. Information Systems Organization and Personnel Inventory and Assessment

    E. Current Information Systems Plans Inventory and Assessment

Appendixes

    Inventory of Infrastructure Projects

    Critical Infrastructure Project Definitions

IV. Information Systems Plan

    A. Information Systems Tactical Plan (up to two years)

        1. Project Definitions

        2. Prioritized List of Project Definitions

        3. Schedule

    B. Information Systems Long-Range Plan (two to five years)

        1. Project Definitions

        2. Schedule

    C. Plan Review and Maintenance Guidelines

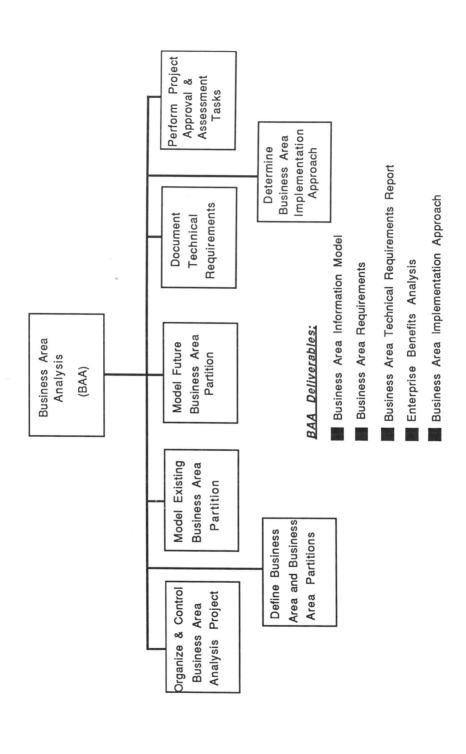

Business Area
Analysis
(BAA)

Organize & Control
Business Area
Analysis Project

Model Existing
Business Area
Partition

Define Business
Area and Business
Area Partitions

Model Future
Business Area
Partition

Document
Technical
Requirements

Perform Project
Approval &
Assessment
Tasks

Determine
Business Area
Implementation
Approach

BAA Deliverables:

■ Business Area Information Model

■ Business Area Requirements

■ Business Area Technical Requirements Report

■ Enterprise Benefits Analysis

■ Business Area Implementation Approach

4

BUSINESS AREA ANALYSIS PHASE

The Information Systems Planning (ISP) phase determines which Business Areas should be the first targets for Business Area Analysis (BAA). The objectives of the BAA phase are to understand what data and processes are necessary to meet enterprise goals and to determine how these data and processes interrelate within the selected Business Area. As a result of this analysis, system solutions are identified and System Design projects are proposed.

Goals

Model the Business Area accurately by developing a fully normalized data model and an activity model, and preserve them in the Information Engineering Workbench Encyclopedia.

Relate Business Area processes to their corresponding Critical Success Factors.

Identify potential design projects and determine priorities by mapping the costs and benefits for each project onto its goals and Critical Success Factors.

Approach

A Business Area Information Model is created to serve as a baseline for subsequent tasks. This model is then partitioned into manageable and technically feasible analysis projects. For each of the partitions, a future model is developed, and an overall strategy to design systems for these models is established. A fully normalized data model is developed; the functions identified in ISP are decomposed into processes; a data flow diagram is developed to show how the processes interrelate; and a matrix is built to show what data entities are used, updated, and created, as well as through what processes.

Deliverables

Business Area Information Model
      Normalized Entity Model
      Process Specifications
      Business Event Identification
Business Area Requirements
Business Area Technical Requirements Report
Enterprise Benefits Analysis
Business Area Implementation Proposal

Considerations

Information Systems Planning, the previous phase of Information Engineering, is dedicated to defining and documenting the enterprise and its strategic directions, and to ensuring that the results of the BAA meet corporate needs. If an Information Systems Plan has not been completed, a brief plan should be developed to create a rough-cut enterprise model.

The reconciliation of one partition to another, of a partition to a Business Area, and of Future to Current Business Area Information Models is best carried out recursively and heuristically. Thus the sequence of events described for this phase is not strictly linear. For practical reasons, design projects may be started before all partitions are completely studied, if sufficient information is known about all relevant partitions and their interconnections.

The success and efficiency of the System Design phase depend heavily on a thorough analysis of the relevant Business Area. The efficiency improvements possible through the use of code generators and other Fourth-Generation Languages are especially dependent on this.

ORGANIZE AND CONTROL BUSINESS AREA ANALYSIS PROJECT

The management tasks identified for this phase reflect the general activities and responsibilities of project management. To initiate and manage the project, perform the following tasks:

Organize and train the project team;

Develop and revise the work unit plan;

Review actual versus planned activities;

Review work products;

Analyze the consistency of project definitions and the proposed design;

Evaluate change requests;

Review and revise control procedures;

Report on project status;

Perform short-interval scheduling.

DEFINE BUSINESS AREA AND BUSINESS AREA PARTITIONS

The purpose of this activity is to lay the foundation for the rest of the BAA project. The primary objective is to establish a Business Area Information Model that reflects enterprise strategy and defines the scope of the BAA project. This baseline model guides the BAA and serves as a reconciliation benchmark for subsequent tasks.

This activity divides the Business Area into partitions that are manageable and cohesive, and that form a logical group of related business activities. A Business Area partition project is defined by the Business Area Information Model associated with it.

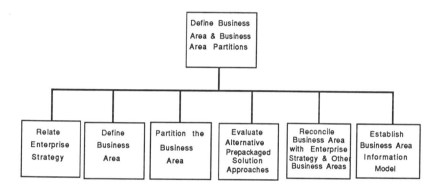

Relate Enterprise Strategy

The purpose of this task is to relate the strategic directions of the enterprise to the Business Area under study and to ensure that the results of the BAA meet corporate needs. Under optimal circumstances, the BAA can use the strategic information developed during the Information Systems Plan phase. However, if an Information Systems Plan has not been prepared, it will be necessary to conduct a quick analysis of enterprise strategy. This analysis should cover the main points of the ISP phase.

To understand the enterprise and its information needs, identify:

Organizational Units

Locations

Goals

Critical Success Factors

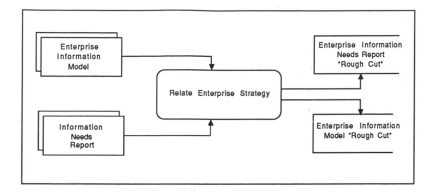

Critical Assumptions

Strategic Information Needs

Technical Directions.

Develop an initial Enterprise Information Model by identifying high-level Subject Areas and major Business Functions. The model should encompass relationships between:

Subject Areas and Organizational Units

Subject Areas and Locations

Business Functions and Organizational Units

Business Functions and Locations

Subject Areas and Critical Success Factors

Business Functions and Goals

Business Functions and Critical Success Factors

Goals and Critical Success Factors

Goals and Entities

Goals and Organization Units.

Define Business Area

A high-level model is developed to establish the domain of the Business Area. The relevant information for this task may be available from the ISP study. In this case, it is still important to verify the information received.

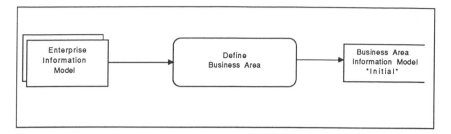

To gain a broader understanding of the environment, develop a Business Area Information Model similar to the one suggested in the "Relate Enterprise Strategy" task, but extended to a deeper level. Drive business activities down to processes and Subject Areas down to entity types; identify the key attributes of entity types; and identify existing data files and systems.

Identify requirements by driving the strategic Critical Success Factors and goals down one level. Relate the Critical Success Factors and goals to the organizational units they support, and interview functional (line) managers to determine lower level goals and Critical Success Factors.

Extend the Enterprise Information Model by defining new entity types, attributes, relationships, and business activities. Integrate these at the lowest level of the activity model. Finally, add the new definitions to the entity model and to the business activity model.

Partition the Business Area

It is often useful, from a management standpoint, to divide the Business Area into logical groupings of processes and entity types that can be studied as separate analysis projects. Such partitioning is required due to the size of the Business Area, resource constraints, time constraints, and other situational factors.

Define Business Area partitions by clustering the Business Area objects (such as Critical Success Factors, entity types, and Business Functions) to determine the most logical groupings, based on the strength of relationships between entity types. Determine Business Area Information Model partitions by relating the current model to the Business Area partitions. Also develop Business Area project definitions.

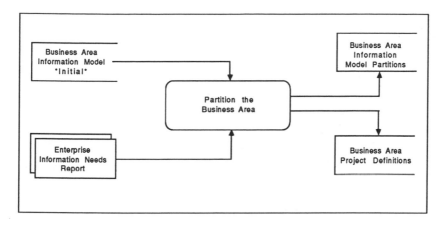

Evaluate Alternative Prepackaged Solution Approaches

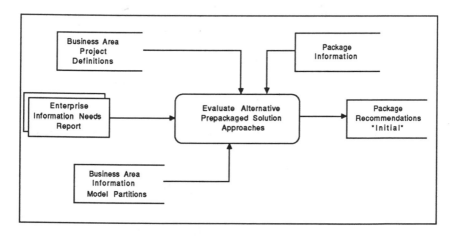

The purpose of this task is to assess the suitability of prepackaged solutions (e.g., vendor packages, Fourth-Generation Languages, Decision Support Systems, and expert systems) for the Business Area Information Model or for any of its partitions. To complete this task, assess the marketplace for packaged products; do a rough fit of packaged product functions and data against the Business Area Information Model; and identify potential Business Area Information Model partitions that are appropriate for a prepackaged solution.

Reconcile Business Area with Enterprise Strategy and Other Business Areas

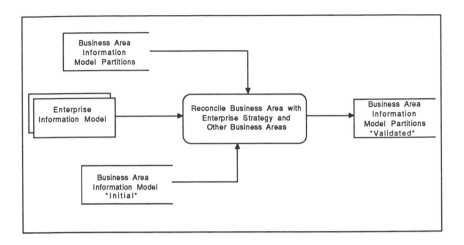

The identified Business Area partitions must support enterprise strategy and integrate with other Business Areas. To ensure that they do, use a matrix of "Business Activities versus Critical Success Factors" to determine the correlation between the given Business Area partition and the Critical Success Factors identified in enterprise strategy. Also compare the model of the given Business Area with those thus far completed for all other Business Areas, and resolve any redundancies, inconsistencies, or conflicts. Repeat this process for each partition in the Business Area.

Establish Business Area Information Model

The purpose of this task is to establish the baseline information model for the Business Area. This model will guide the BAA and serve as a reconciliation benchmark. This is the final task for this activity, because it is first necessary to study the Business Area before deciding on a baseline Business Area Information Model. An industry standard model could be used. Otherwise, the Business Area Information Model and the Enterprise Information Model should be refined to serve as a baseline model.

Begin by locating an existing model that can facilitate the Business Area projects. These models can exist in various formats, including

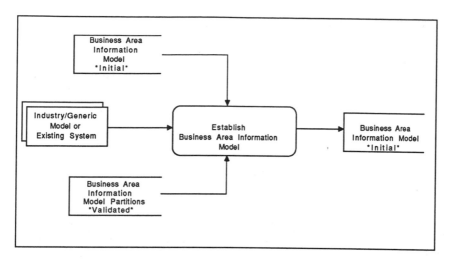

industry information models, generic information models, and models of existing information systems. If an adequate existing model is not available, the current Business Area Information Model and Enterprise Information Model should serve as the baseline model for the project. Enhance and organize the Business Area Information Model so it can be used as the project continues.

MODEL EXISTING BUSINESS AREA PARTITION

To understand the current environment and to verify this understanding with the user, it is necessary to build a model of this environment within each Business Area partition. This model also serves as a basis for defining the future system.

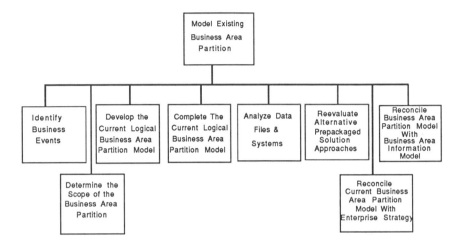

Identify Business Events

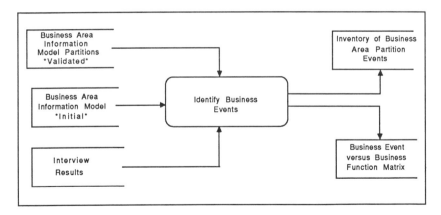

This task's purpose is to analyze events within the Business Area. Business events tie together enterprise activities, data, and technologies to respond to the environment. Business events are easily verified by users. They provide guidance for decomposing the business activity model, and they serve as a basis for identifying logical transactions in the model.

To identify external events, evaluate the Business Area entity-relationship model (from ISP) for events that create entities and relationships. Develop an initial event list that includes the person(s) responsible for the event and the process responding to it. (Analyze the enterprise organizational chart to identify the individuals responsible.) Identifying events and the individuals responsible for a given process will reveal candidates for the first set of interviews.

Interview users according to the preliminary event list. Data and process names should reflect the views of the interviewee. Terms that are not clearly understandable must be defined separately. Also, reports that are received (or sent) should be collected and placed in the work papers as samples.

Develop a data flow model identifying external agents and their data flows in the activity context. Prepare two entity-relationship diagrams: one with a "before view," showing entities and relationships prior to the activity, and one with an "after view," showing entity types and relationships resulting from the activity.

Analyze, change, and extend the designated Subject Area of the Enterprise Information Model by adding to the entity-relationship diagram any entity types or relationships identified during user interviews. For each entity type, add attributes within the Subject Area. Define all new entity types, attributes, and relationships. Associate events with the business activity model to identify logical transactions. Finally, create a matrix to illustrate the relationship between events and business activities.

Determine the Scope of the Business Area Partition

This task is performed to determine the externals and all flows of data within the scope of the Business Area partition.

When you have completed the interviews, construct a context diagram to represent the domain of the Business Area partition. Examine each activity model to determine the external agents with respect to the scope of the project. All flows of data and reports from activity models to or from external agents should be included in the diagram, while all flows from activity models to other externals within the scope of the system should be omitted. (This diagram typically looks like a pin cushion.)

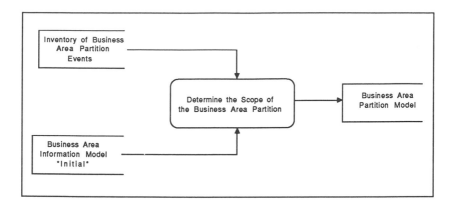

The logical context diagram will include the name of the Business Area partition, the external agents around the Business Area partition, and the data flow components to and from the respective external agents. This is an appropriate time to reevaluate project scope in terms of the number of entity types, the relationships, and the categories of data flowing into the Business Area. This further level of detail will indicate whether the original scope has been exceeded.

Develop the Current Logical Business Area Partition Model

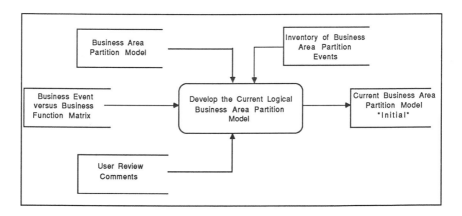

Develop the Current Logical Business Area Partition Model to provide a view of the entity types and activities currently maintained within the Business Area partition. This is the basis for identifying additional system requirements by modifying and adding to the Business Area Information Model.

Build a process model to provide a complete decomposition of all the business activities within the Business Area partition. Concentrate on the activity itself, not on its current implementation. Develop a decomposition diagram to show the logical breakdown of business processes.

Group activities into similar categories, using the Business Area decomposition diagram developed during the ISP project, and then decompose the grouped activities. A logically partitioned Business Area will be the end result.

Review the lowest level diagrams with users to determine if functional primitives have been identified, based on the depth and scope of the project. Correct any diagrams, taking care not to introduce physical characteristics identified via user review. To ensure consistency, it is very important that corrections are made at the highest level diagram first and allowed to ripple through to lower levels. The review of lower level diagrams with users will further refine the logical models and determine if the function of the logical model is congruent with the interview results.

Complete the Current Logical Business Area Partition Model

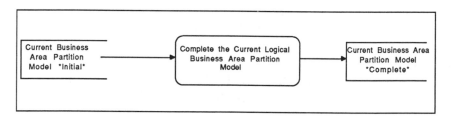

To complete the development of the Current Logical Business Area Partition Model, build entity models for each data flow and for each functional primitive. Then build process specifications for each functional primitive using action diagrams.

Analyze Data Files and Systems

Data files and systems must be analyzed to associate the current automation environment within the Business Area with the current Business Area Information Model. This will assist in the assessment of migration to the future model and will identify strengths and weaknesses within the existing systems.

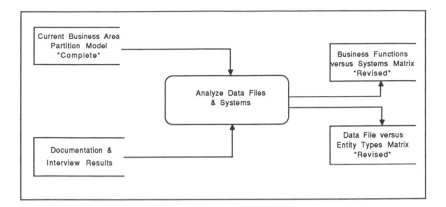

Using the matrices identified in the high-level Business Area Information Model, produce revised matrices of "Business Activities versus Systems" and "Data Files versus Entity Types." Evaluate the quality of data maintained within the Business Area, based on the information needs assessed during the Information Systems Planning phase. Consider factors such as correctness, completeness, and timeliness.

This evaluation can have great significance in estimating conversion requirements, evaluating prepackaged solution approaches, and assigning priority to Business Area projects. Significant effort should not be devoted to this task, however, unless the associations are considered essential for migration to the Future Business Area Information Model. Continue developing the matrix diagrams already established by adding business activities, systems, data files, and entity types.

Reevaluate Alternative Prepackaged Solution Approaches

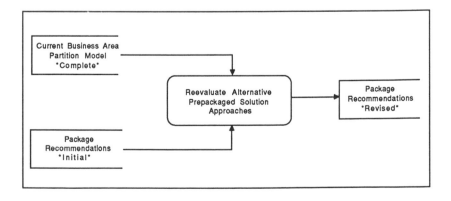

The purpose of this task is to address the applicability of prepackaged solutions for solving BAA problems. The reasons for using or not using a packaged approach may become clearer as more detailed information is known about the Business Area and its current data files and systems.

Review previous package recommendations from the "Evaluate Alternative Prepackaged Solution Approaches" task; assess the marketplace for available packaged products; and do a rough fit of packaged product functions and data against the Business Area Information Model.

Reconcile Current Business Area Partition Model with Enterprise Strategy

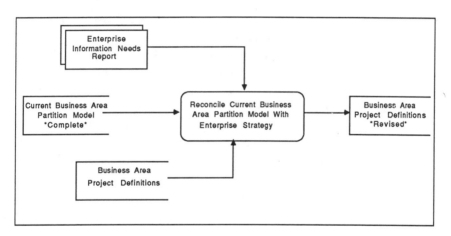

Reconcile the Current Business Area Partition Model with enterprise strategy to determine the extent of change needed within the current environment to meet enterprise goals. Analyze the relationship between enterprise information resources (such as business activities, systems, and data files) and enterprise Critical Success Factors. Determine to what extent the Current Business Area Partition Model supports enterprise strategy, and revise Business Area project definitions, if necessary.

Reconcile Business Area Partition Model with Business Area Information Model

This task is performed to ensure that the Business Area Partition Model follows the guidelines established by the Business Area Information

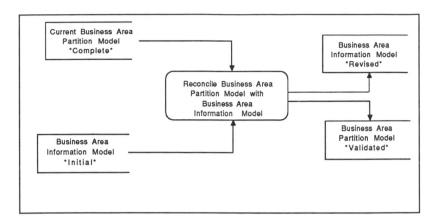

Model and that this baseline is updated to reflect the requirements of the Business Area partition under study.

Begin by comparing the Business Area partition to the Business Area Information Model baseline. Then compare this partition with the other Business Area partitions examined thus far, and resolve any differences.

Update the baseline to incorporate the features of the examined Business Area partitions. If separate encyclopedias are used for different partitions, reconciling differences between encyclopedias may surface contradictions in Critical Success Factors. In such instances, these contradictions need to be resolved.

MODEL FUTURE BUSINESS AREA PARTITION

In this activity, requirements are identified for Business Area partitions and incorporated into the Future Business Area Information Model.

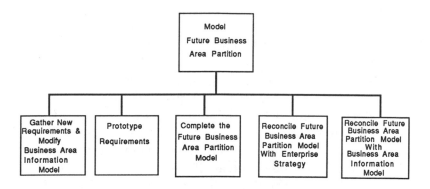

Gather New Requirements and Modify Business Area Information Model

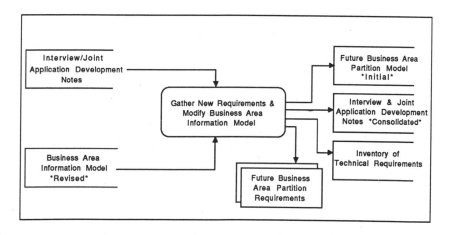

The purpose of this task is to identify requirements for improving the ability of the Business Area to meet the goals and Critical Success Factors of the enterprise that are not currently reflected in the Business Area Information Model.

To accomplish this task, decompose goals and Critical Success Factors into future Business Area partition requirements that will meet the goals and Critical Success Factors defined for the given Business

Area partition. Organize lower level goals and Critical Success Factors under parent goals and Critical Success Factors.

Identify changes to the Current Business Area Information Model, and assess the changes required to the model. These changes might include additional entity types and relationships; additional attributes; and additional, modified, or deleted business activities.

Build an initial Future Business Area Information Model to produce a preliminary future model. To build an initial Future Business Area Information Model, revise the process view and revise the entity view, adding new entity types, attributes, and relationships. Populate the initial future model with all of the attributes of the current model.

One strategy for populating the future entity view is to use the attributes extracted from the inputs, outputs, and physical files from the current mechanisms and data collections. Note that this population may update the future model with attributes that it does not need. Any redundancy will be removed later in the "Reconcile Future Business Area Partition Model with Business Area Information Model" task.

Prototype Requirements

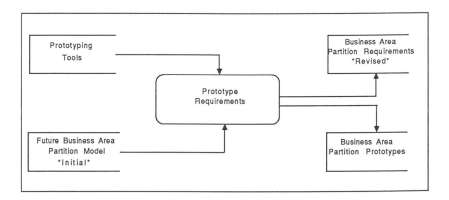

Prototyping helps to enhance both user involvement and the refinement of future Business Area partition requirements. It also helps to define external requirements, such as for screens and reports, and to pass along a working prototype to the Design and Construction phases. The overall process involves selecting a prototyping tool, developing prototypes, iteratively reviewing them with users, and refining requirements definitions.

Complete the Future Business Area Partition Model

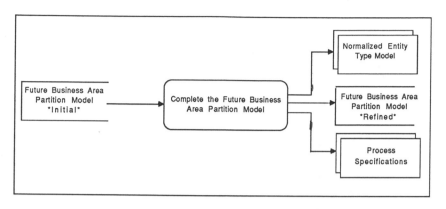

This task is performed to complete the Future Business Area Partition Model by specifying processes and by modeling their behavior in terms of the conditions and sequences under which they operate. It is also performed to ensure that the process model supports all transactions and that the entity type model supports all business activities.

Begin by refining the Future Business Area Partition Model. Decompose each bottom level activity into a data flow diagram fragment. To ensure that the entity type model satisfies the activity model, create views of the entity type model for each process on the data flow diagram fragment; refine the entity type model views by adding or deleting entity types and attributes; consolidate the entity type model views to form the Future Business Area Partition Entity Type Model; and define all new entity types, attributes, and relationships.

Make certain the process model supports the entity model by associating events and entities to show creation, retrieval, update, and deletion processes. Also, refine the future entity type model by normalizing it, by adding volumes to it for sizing purposes, and by adding volumes to events. In the Information Engineering Workbench, use the Action Diagrammer to specify processes by building detailed specifications for each process on the data flow diagram fragments.

Reconcile Future Business Area Partition Model with Enterprise Strategy

To ensure that the future system supports the information needs of the enterprise, analyze the relationship between the Future Business Area

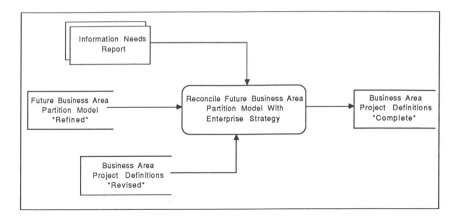

Partition Model objects (e.g., entity types, business activities, and processes) and enterprise Critical Success Factors and goals. Determine to what extent the model supports enterprise strategy, and refine the Future Business Area Partition Model, if necessary.

Reconcile Future Business Area Partition Model with Business Area Information Model

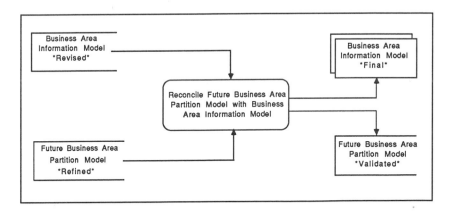

This task is performed to ensure that the Future Business Area Partition Model follows the guidelines established by the baseline Business Area Information Model and that the baseline model is updated to reflect the requirements of the Business Area partition. Compare the future Business Area partition to the baseline model and resolve any differences. Update the baseline model to incorporate the features of the Future Business Area Partition Model. Finally, reconcile redundant attributes between the Future Business Area Information Model and the baseline model.

DOCUMENT TECHNICAL REQUIREMENTS

The purpose of this activity is to identify common technical requirements within a given Business Area; that is, those requirements oriented to more than a single partition. This activity does not address
hardware and software requirements. That will be accomplished in the
next activity, "Determine Business Area Implementation Approach,"
when more is known about the implementation approach. This activity
focuses on determining issues and constraints such as volume, performance, and security requirements.

If there is more than one partition in the Business Area, the technical
requirements for previously studied Business Area partitions should be
considered along with the requirements for this partition. Also, what-
ever is currently known about the technical requirements of partitions
still not completely studied should also be included.

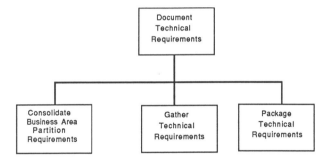

Consolidate Business Area Partition Requirements

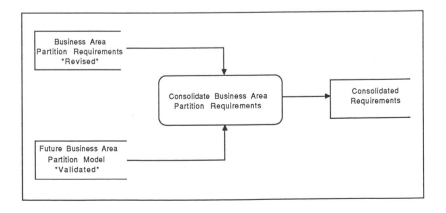

If there are multiple partitions within a given Business Area, this task is performed to group all Business Area requirements to analyze the overlap in technical requirements, and to analyze the requirements for consistency. To carry out this task, group requirements based on similar function, similar technical aspects, and similar Critical Success Factor support.

Gather Technical Requirements

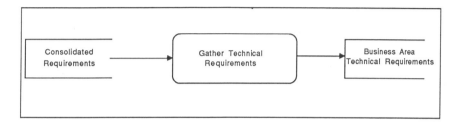

This task is performed to identify the combined technical requirements and constraints for the new systems, and to determine the technical resources needed. To accomplish this task, determine security and auditability requirements that might affect the resources needed for the new systems. Also determine performance and volume requirements.

Package Technical Requirements

From the list of technical requirements for the Business Area, prepare a formal document outlining the technical resources required to implement Business Area projects.

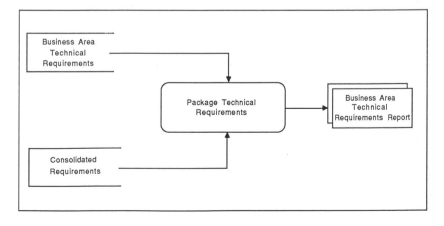

DETERMINE BUSINESS AREA IMPLEMENTATION APPROACH

The purpose of this activity is to establish the technical strategy and management plans for implementing the Business Area requirements. Automation boundaries are set, solution approaches are determined, and hardware and software requirements are identified. Plans are then justified through a benefits analysis and a report is packaged documenting the implementation approach.

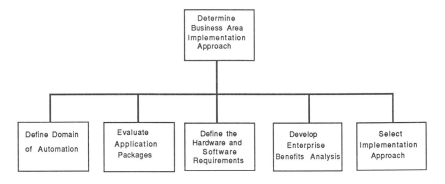

Define Domain of Automation

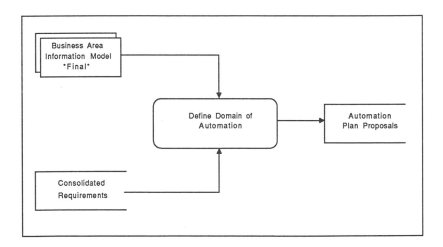

Define the domain of automation to establish candidate external interface boundaries and the scope of the automated system. To accomplish this, analyze the consolidated requirements and the consolidated Business Area Information Model to set the boundaries for automation.

Scope may be determined by a number of factors, including the relation of projects to enterprise Critical Success Factors, the quality of integration among projects, the technical resources available for projects, and cost factors. Partition the Business Area into system solution portions and manual solution portions.

Evaluate Application Packages

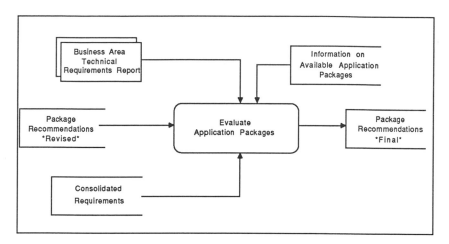

It is important to determine whether a system required for any Business Area project can be purchased rather than built to specification. To determine this, review previous package recommendations and analyze the functional and technical requirements for the Business Area and its partitions. Then review automation plan proposals, review the marketplace for applicable packages, and evaluate the candidate packages.

Define the Hardware and Software Requirements

The purpose of this task is to determine the hardware and software architecture needed for the new system(s). Determine the resources needed based on data from the Information Systems Profile Report produced during the Information Systems Planning phase. Such resources might include:

Hardware systems (mainframe, mini, and micro);
Networking and distribution plans, if applicable;

System volume and performance requirements;
Database and telecommunications software;
System or packaged software;
Specialized peripheral equipment.

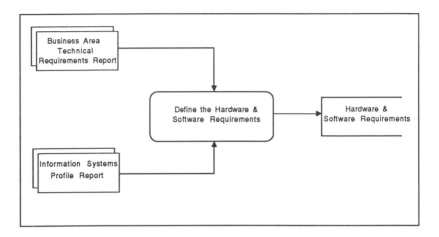

Develop Enterprise Benefits Analysis

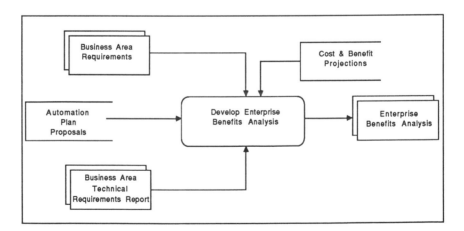

An enterprise benefits analysis is performed to determine the cultural, financial, and technical impact the future systems will have on the enterprise.

Determine the cultural effect by assessing the impact of the proposed domain of automation on the enterprise. Assess the enterprise culture to determine the policy regarding the introduction of new technology and its effect on work practices. Assess the level of computer literacy within the Business Area, identify the types of people who will use the new systems, and assess the need for education. Relate the findings to the domain of automation.

Determine the technical effect by assessing the changes that need to be made in the enterprise's technical environment. To do this, describe the technical environment for each domain, and estimate the personnel resources needed to support the environment.

Determine the financial effect by assessing the costs and benefits for each domain of automation. Produce a rough-cut implementation and operation cost estimate for each domain, associate the cost with enterprise goals and Critical Success Factors, and produce a rough-cut benefit projection for each domain.

Select Implementation Approach

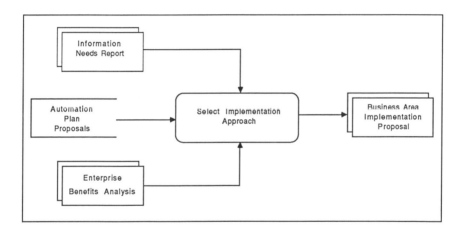

This task is performed to outline the Business Area design concept and the benefits and impact of automating the Business Area. Begin by selecting an appropriate domain of automation and subdividing it into design partitions. These may or may not correspond to Business Area partitions.

Use the enterprise benefit analysis results and your knowledge of the user environment to select the most appropriate domain of automation. Partition the domain of automation by clustering activities into candidate design partitions. Assess the partitioning in relation to the prioritized goals and Critical Success Factors. Also, identify the technical implementation sequence, assess the speed with which the design partitions may be implemented in light of the goals and Critical Success Factors, and select the best design partitioning. Finally, develop an initial, high-level Systems Design Plan, including brief design project descriptions, and prepare a report.

PERFORM PROJECT APPROVAL AND ASSESSMENT TASKS

To perform the approval and assessment tasks required to complete a Business Area Analysis phase project, obtain approvals for phase deliverables, and assess the performance of project team members.

BUSINESS AREA ANALYSIS DELIVERABLES

    I. Business Area Information Model
       A. Inventory of Business Area Partition Events
       B. Normalized Entity Type Model
       C. Process Specifications
       D. Current Business Area Partition Model
       E. Future Business Area Partition Model
   II. Business Area Requirements
       A. Future Business Area Partition Requirements
       B. Consolidated Requirements
      Appendix
         Business Area Partition Prototypes
  III. Business Area Technical Requirements Report
  IV. Enterprise Benefits Analysis
       A. Cultural Impact
       B. Technical Impact
       C. Financial Impact
   V. Business Area Implementation Approach
       A. Design Concept Proposal
       B. Initial Systems Design Plan
      Appendixes
         Automation Plan Proposals
         Package Recommendations
         Hardware and Software Requirements

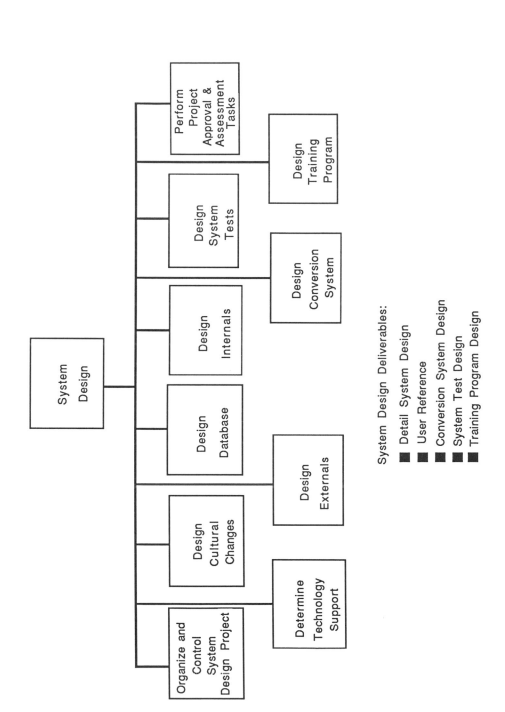

System Design

- Organize and Control System Design Project
- Design Cultural Changes
- Design Externals
- Design Database
- Design Internals
- Design Conversion System
- Design System Tests
- Perform Project Approval & Assessment Tasks
- Design Training Program
- Determine Technology Support

System Design Deliverables:

- Detail System Design
- User Reference
- Conversion System Design
- System Test Design
- Training Program Design

5

SYSTEM DESIGN PHASE

System Design is the third phase of the Information Engineering process. During System Design, Business Area requirements are transformed into detailed application system specifications.

Goals

Ensure that the software being designed supports the goals of the enterprise by supporting the Critical Success Factors associated with the relevant Business Area.

Provide a seamless transition from analysis by transforming the models developed in Business Area Analysis into design specifications.

Ensure that designers will satisfy user requirements by using prototypes and the User Reference as communication tools.

Enhance project quality and communication between project team members by using standard models and well documented work steps.

Give the user a strong influence over the external design.

Detail the system conversion procedures, user and operator training program, test design and user acceptance criteria, and implementation strategy.

Approach

A framework for design is created by determining the overall technological support for the project and any cultural changes necessary to support the new system.

The design of externals and of the database both precedes and sets the target for internal design. Thus design proceeds smoothly since items such as screen and report layouts are in place prior to designing the programs. If a code generator is used, the transition between external and internal design is much tighter and is made more automatically. This establishes a basis for iterative development using prototypes. Prototyping is useful for communicating effectively with users; and when this approach is coupled with a code generator, the time required for design and construction can be decreased dramatically while improving the quality of the resulting application.

Finally, the conversion system and procedures; the system test script, cases, and acceptance process; and the training program are designed.

Deliverables

Detail System Design

User Reference

Conversion System Design

System Test Design

Training Program Design

Considerations

To avoid design drift, care should be taken to map design elements back to the Critical Success Factors associated with the corresponding Business Area.

Decisions concerning the development environment are made early in this phase, so that the system design can be tailored to the hardware and software that will be used. As part of this effort, the use of a code generator and/or other software aids to support rapid development should be evaluated against the costs of longer development cycles using hand coding approaches.

GAMMA, the code generator from KnowledgeWare, Inc., has the ability to insulate the developer from the target technical environment. By altering parameters in a code generator, like GAMMA, parts of a system generated for one DBMS environment can be regenerated for another. In general, code generators are powerful aids in the design and construction of new systems, and should be used unless offsetting factors prevent their use. Throughout this phase and the next, GAMMA is used to illustrate how a code generator can be utilized for developing systems. Obviously, other generators would have somewhat different capabilities.

In addition to generating code, code generators organize and document other information pertaining to the system under development. For example, GAMMA's Design Manual includes programming products such as files, screens, and reports, as well as documentary products that are expressed in a narrative format (e.g., introductions and appendixes). Thus the Design Manual serves as an automated set of workpapers created as a byproduct of task execution. At all times, it reflects what has been done and what is left to do on the project.

Using this approach, the Construction and System Design phases can proceed in parallel. For example, after a subsystem is designed, it can be constructed while other subsystems are being designed. Prototypes can be turned over to construction on a subsystem-by-subsystem basis. Also, the conversion system can be constructed and tested during System Design.

In the System Design phase, many of the activities may be performed concurrently. Thus the sequence of System Design activities does not imply a temporal order. However, within each activity, the task sequence does imply a temporal order, and the tasks should be performed sequentially.

ORGANIZE AND CONTROL SYSTEM DESIGN PROJECT

The management tasks identified for this phase reflect the general activities and responsibilities of project management. To initiate and manage the project, perform the following tasks:

Organize and train the project team;

Develop and revise the work unit plan;

Review actual versus planned activities;

Review work products;

Analyze the consistency of project definitions and the proposed design;

Evaluate change requests;

Review and revise control procedures;

Report on project status;

Perform short-interval scheduling.

DETERMINE TECHNOLOGY SUPPORT

The purpose of this activity is to define the construction and installation operating environments and the approaches to be used to build the system. These issues need to be addressed here, since they may have a substantial influence on the approach to system design. During the Construction phase, a development environment that facilitates system building is needed. This environment must offer the appropriate mix of development tools (code generators and Fourth-Generation Languages) and test tools (test data generators and file compare utilities), supported by appropriate control and management procedures.

The installation environment requirements are typically identical to those of the operational system; the emphasis shifts from development and test software to sufficient hardware to meet performance and storage demands, supplemented by backup and recovery software. Of course, control and management procedures play a significant role in this environment as well. In particular, installation strategies (such as phased, abrupt cutover, or parallel runs) can have a substantial impact on the amount and timing of technological support.

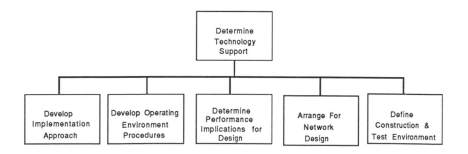

Develop Implementation Approach

The approach for implementation and the options and sequence for design, construction, and installation work are established in this task. To complete this task, validate the preliminary implementation decision (made in Business Area Analysis) to use a code generator, Fourth-Generation Language, or other programming language. Determine

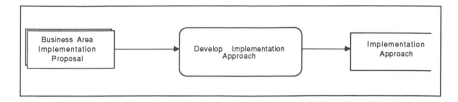

whether to define internal transactions or external transactions first. Determine the installation options and cutover design (e.g, phased, by location, by subsystem, by function, or by parallel operation). Also determine whether to modify and extend the prototypes that were built to reveal requirements during the Business Area Analysis phase.

Finally, confirm the technical specifications from Business Area Analysis, including the hardware "centralization versus decentralization" decision and the computer size selection decision.

If GAMMA is to be used on the project, make arrangements to acquire the product and have it installed. If GAMMA is available during System Design, the project team can make maximum use of the power of GAMMA's documentary and programming products. At this time, determine the GAMMA System Control Set and the Boilerplate file. This will result in the "Define Construction and Test Environment" task to be executed in parallel with this task in order to establish the System Control Set.

Develop Operating Environment Procedures

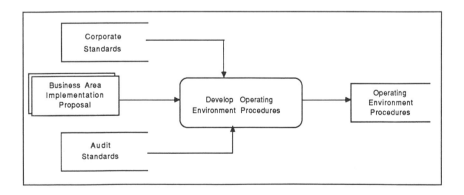

Control procedures must be established for the operational environment. This requires the development of procedures for normal system startup and shutdown, database backup and maintenance, restart and recovery, and security and audit.

Determine Performance Implications for Design

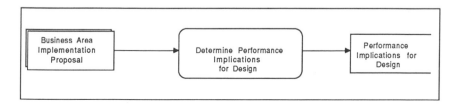

The purpose of this task is to make designers aware of the implications of application-specific performance requirements on the design of the new system. This is accomplished by translating the performance requirements specified during the Business Area Analysis phase into a set of quantifiable impacts on Central Processing Unit cycles, line speeds, transaction volumes, printing volumes, and storage needs (by media) over time. If necessary, conduct performance analysis modeling studies on the existing data center equipment and other candidate hardware/software configurations.

Arrange for Network Design

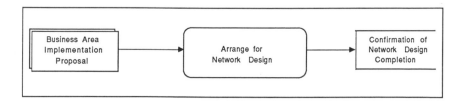

Notify the network specialist to establish the data communications environment for the new system. Provide this individual with performance specifications (i.e., volumes, frequencies, transmission characteristics, and peak load times) and location specifications. In addition, provide input on whether the system should share an existing network or whether it requires a new one for security or other application requirement reasons. The network specialist may determine that a new network is needed, based on overall traffic studies, or that enhancements to the existing network are required.

Define Construction and Test Environment

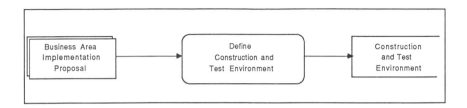

The construction and test environment is defined to determine the facilities to be used by the construction and test teams. Determine the hardware and software system(s) to be used for conversion, construction, and testing. These may or may not be the same as the operational target system. Determine the development aids and administrative support to be used. Define and document the control procedures to be used in the construction and test environment. These include test library controls and migration procedures, and software authorization and usage controls. If GAMMA is used on the project, this task should be completed in parallel with the "Develop Implementation Approach" task.

DESIGN CULTURAL CHANGES

The purpose of this activity is to develop a plan to accommodate the cultural changes (such as in organizational structure, skill and staffing levels, job content, policies, and procedures) required to implement the new system. The apparent cultural changes may have been identified during the Business Area Analysis phase; however, these should be carefully reevaluated here (situations may have changed within user areas) before being included in a formal plan.

Because this activity may involve making significant changes within user areas, high-level user management should actively participate in the design and approval of this work. Ideally, they should assume responsibility for this activity, although some of the work will need to be accomplished by information systems professionals, as well as by organizational design specialists and human resource specialists.

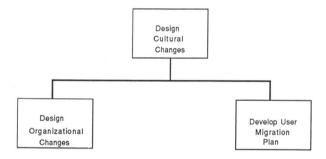

Design Organizational Changes

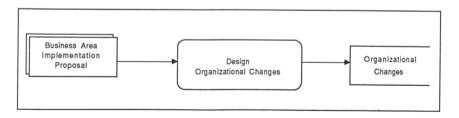

In this task, adjust existing organizational units, where necessary, to gain optimal benefits from the installation of a new system. Given the procedural changes planned in conjunction with the new system, design an organizational structure that provides for the proper skills and numbers of people at the proper locations. Identify organizational entities whose functions will change or will no longer be needed. If a group's function changes significantly, a new charter/mission statement should be developed.

Where required, create new position descriptions and revise existing ones, consistent with current enterprise policies and practices. The extent of user dislocation and organizational disruption should be noted, since it will become a key determinant as to the amount and emphasis of user training required to ensure acceptance of the new system.

Develop User Migration Plan

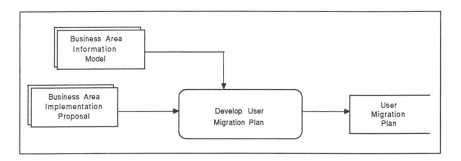

A User Migration Plan is developed to provide a documented plan for the orderly transition of the user organization to a position in which it can benefit most from the new system. Determine the actions that will effect the organizational changes, as well as their sequence and timing. Also determine the projected needs for the acquisition and elimination of resources, the need for relocation of resources; and the schedule, volume (i.e., number of participants and classes), and timing for training.

Determine the preliminary schedule and timing for migration from the current environment to the new system. This should be revisited after the completion of the "Design Conversion System" activity. If this plan is not developed by senior user managers, it is critical to arrange for them to review and revise the plan immediately, until it is approved. Failure to gain early approval can jeopardize a system installation effort.

DESIGN EXTERNALS

The purpose of this activity is to design the automated and human interfaces and the manual activities required to carry out the specified functions. The goals of the external system design are:

To assist users in operating the new system efficiently;

To guide internal developers in determining which functions the system needs to accomplish; and

To guide test case development.

If prototyping was used to bring requirements to the surface during the Business Area Analysis phase, a partial set of externals may already exist. Their continued usefulness to the design effort must be evaluated, subject to criteria such as completeness, accuracy, and consistency with the design scope (which may differ radically from Business Area Analysis). Regardless of whether or not prototypes were inherited from Business Area Analysis, the decision to employ them here also must be tackled; the availability of appropriate software aids and the relative complexity of the user interface are key determinants.

Automated interface design requires thorough communication outside the System Design project's boundaries. Interface data structures, such as files or message formats, must be finalized early in the design. A changing interface specification can frustrate internal design efforts.

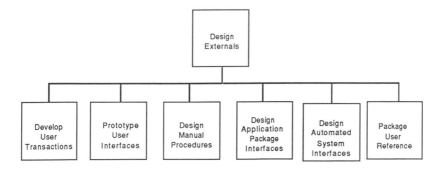

Develop User Transactions

To identify the functional user transactions of the new system, determine the groups of logical functions that the user views as a transaction.

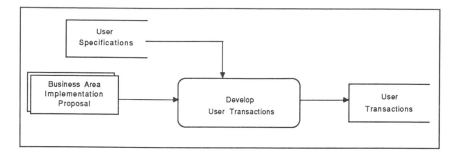

For example, adding a new employee record to a file may be considered one transaction by the user, but may be implemented as several discrete functions internally. Refer to the Business Area Analysis workpapers and existing system documentation for any common functions in user interfaces. This is done in order to ensure consistency of external design across automated systems, as well as to identify existing automated functions which may be used.

Prototype User Interfaces

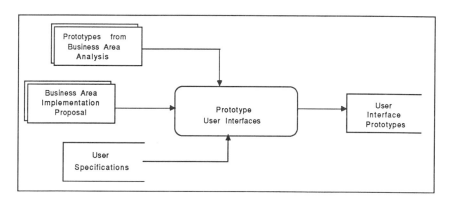

The purpose of this task is to establish the designs needed to support the human interfaces with the new system and to develop the required prototype screens, reports, interactive dialogs, on-line help facilities, and on-line tutorials. If using GAMMA, identify the set of items to be prototyped, and cross reference this list with the prototypes inherited from Business Area Analysis. Develop the first iteration of the prototype, prototyping each screen by first building the screen products. Using the "Show" option in GAMMA's Screen Painter panels, adjust alignments and make other model modifications. Prototype reports by building each report product.

If using GAMMA, test screen prototypes using the "Prototype" option in the Execution Functions Sub-Menu. Once the list of screen products appears, select the appropriate product and the "RUN" option to simulate data entry, basic editing, error handling, and screen switching. Test report prototypes by writing and executing simple report driver program products.

Finally, review the prototype with users. Add user-identified enhancements or corrections, and repeat testing until the users are satisfied. However, before acting on significant enhancement requests, it is important to consider their impact on internal design activities that use the externals as a baseline. Verify that in an effort to meet user expectations, project scope is not inadvertently expanded without proper authorization.

Design Manual Procedures

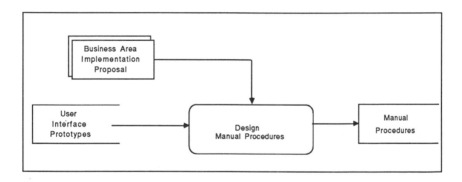

This task is performed to design the manual procedures for the new system and to provide users, data center personnel, and operators with guidance for successful operation of the new system. Review the Business Area Analysis domain of automation to identify the functions outside the automated boundary. Meet with user management to assign individuals to procedures for which users are responsible. Develop procedures that conform with existing enterprise standards and conventions; and, together with user and data center management, verify their completeness, correctness, and consistency (including how well they mesh with existing procedures that will not change). Also determine the media (paper or electronic) for each procedure.

Design Application Package Interfaces

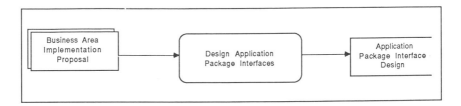

The purpose of this task is to design the interfaces for the application packages that will be incorporated into the system design. The impact, if any, of the packages on external interfaces must be determined. Identify the new system's external interfaces that are to be handled by the package, and assemble the external design documentation for the package. Determine if the package interface is to become a system external interface or if the package screens and reports must be modified or entirely hidden from the users because of inconsistency with other externals, violation of enterprise standards, or for technical reasons (such as overhead or interfacing difficulties). Finally, develop the interfaces from the package externals to the system externals.

Design Automated System Interfaces

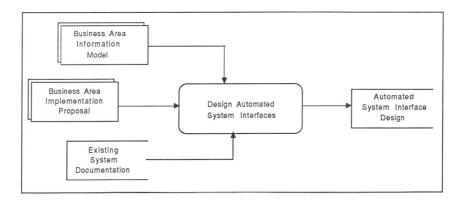

This task is performed to develop an interface design that will transfer information between the new system and existing automated systems. Determine the methods and protocols, transfer media, and data format for each automated system interface. An automated interface may have been designed earlier, if, as a result of the "Design Application Packages Interfaces" task, it was determined that an application package would be used but that the package externals would not be. If so, verify that this previous interface design does not conflict with the interfaces designed here.

In GAMMA, interfaces to other systems may be specified as file, table, and program products. For each interface, specifications are entered into GAMMA's Narrative, General Information, and Notes panels. After entering data definitions into the Data Dictionary, these are transferred to the Data Definition panels for each file product. If appropriate, coordinate with the network specialist to ensure that the automated interfaces are compatible with data communications network requirements and constraints.

Package User Reference

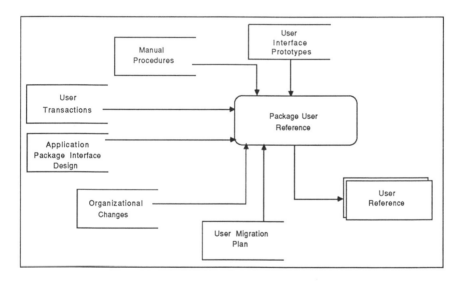

At this time, assemble and organize User Reference materials, and review them with users. Revise these documents as required to obtain the necessary approvals.

DESIGN DATABASE

The purpose of this activity is to translate the Business Area data model into a production database structure. This translation process begins with the gathering of the entity-relationship diagram and the attributed entity descriptions that were developed during Business Area Analysis. Typically, this information will be in Third Normal Form. This model is mapped against the user transactions defined in the "Develop User Transactions" task. In this way, preliminary database access paths can be charted. This input allows a database structure design and physical database design to be developed.

If the system is to be distributed across multiple physical locations, a distributed database may be required. If this is the case, close coordination with enterprise data administration is essential. This very complex task can significantly affect the quality of the design and introduce performance, reliability, availability, recoverability, and security problems if not completed by experienced database designers.

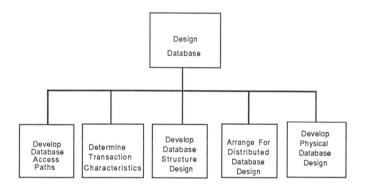

Develop Database Access Paths

Database access paths are developed to depict how data is used by each defined user transaction and to determine the navigational or access paths through the logical data model. Determine how data is accessed in the database. For each transaction, identify the data elements that must be read, updated, inserted, and deleted on the logical data model. At this point, develop a data navigation diagram from the logical data model that depicts navigational paths. Identify the key values on the logical data model for that transaction and the starting entity

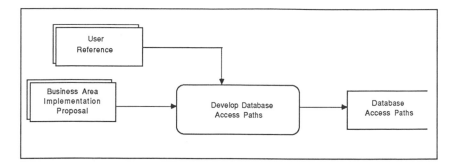

or entry point for the data accesses and their access keys and attributes. Navigational paths are not relevant to the logical design of a relational database and are only useful in physical design to determine keys and indexes.

Determine Transaction Characteristics

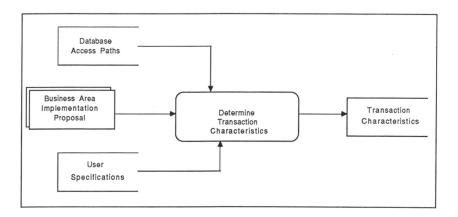

The volumes, frequencies, and response requirements for transaction access to the database are established in this task. Record the volumes from the Hardware and Software Requirements formulated in Business Area Analysis. Determine the peak volumes by grouping transactions with similar volumes together and ranking the groups according to those with the highest volume to those with the lowest. Next, determine the frequency of access to the database and the user response requirements for each transaction. In carrying out this task, refer back to the "Determine Performance Implications for Design" task, and to the previous design of the transactions that will be installed on the same operating system, and fold in their transaction requirements.

Develop Database Structure Design

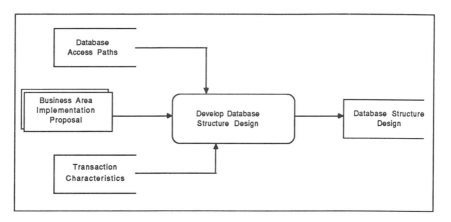

This task provides for the transition from the logical data model to the physical database structure (schema) and identifies the user views of the database (subschema). Determine the general structure of data by identifying the entry point and the relationships between the records. Translate this into a data structure constrained by the technology of the chosen Database Management System.

Develop physical keys and data by translating the logical keys and data on the logical data model to physical keys and data on the database structure. Associate the component to its characteristics by mapping the key and data size of the component, its volume, and its frequency to the database structure. Determine the user view of the data—a logical database that is a subset of the physical database structure.

In GAMMA, record the Database Structure Design as a documentary product; define segments, data groupings, and data elements in the Data Dictionary; and create a GAMMA database product for each database segment.

Arrange for Distributed Database Design

Notify the database specialist (Database Administrator or Database Systems Programmer) to develop a distributed database design if one is required for the new system. The database specialist should be provided with input about data creation and use by organizational unit and/or location.

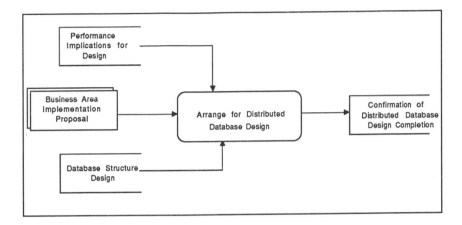

Develop Physical Database Design

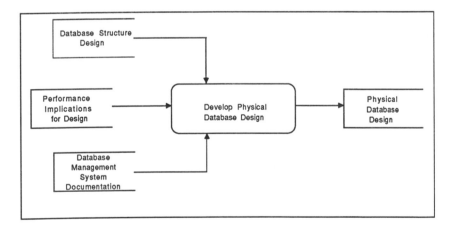

The purpose of this task is to map the Database Structure Design to the physical storage media and to tailor the design for optimal performance. Determine and design the security audit requirements for the database as well as the requirements for recovery/restart. Develop the storage format for the database by grouping the records of different types to take advantage of how the data is used together to process transactions.

Select an access method for the database storage structure, depending on user requirements and the environment.

Using the Performance Implications for Design developed earlier, determine performance possibilities for tuning the database. Identify performance issues for tuning the database storage structure; select an effective block size or control interval size for the storage device; and calculate the database storage requirements to find the size of the physical database. Determine the physical placement on a storage device for the physical database structure by selecting a location on the storage device to minimize contention for the database.

Finally, reassess the database schema/subschema, and make any necessary revisions. Record the schema/subschema into database definitions, using the specific data definition language of the selected Database Management System. (Note that GAMMA does not generate the data definition language statements to define a database for the database manager. For example, in DL/1, GAMMA does not create DBDs. These must be defined outside of GAMMA.) Also record the performance measures for quick access and navigation through the database by identifying the types and numbers of pointers and indexes. In GAMMA, record the database schema/subschema definitions in the Data Dictionary and record the Physical Database Design in the Design Manual as a documentary product. Add physical design details to the General Information panels for each database product.

DESIGN INTERNALS

This activity is performed to develop detailed construction specifications based on the Business Area Information Model created during Business Area Analysis. The internal design is also based on the externals developed during the "Design Externals" activity, which serve as the System Design baseline. The level of detail needed during internal design will be influenced heavily by the target construction environment. With a code generator like GAMMA, a higher level specification is acceptable than if manual coding is to be done. The precision or accuracy of the design is a separate issue from the level of detail. The specifications should be precise enough so that no design decisions need to be made during the Construction phase.

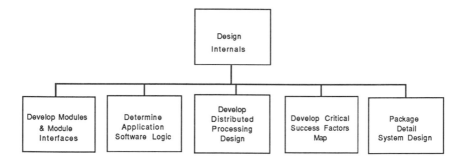

Develop Modules and Module Interfaces

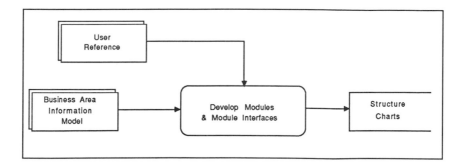

Modules and module interfaces are developed by transforming the data flow diagrams created in Business Area Analysis into a hierarchical structure of program modules. Begin by determining internal transaction design. Determine the transactions by partitioning the processes in the data flow diagrams in the Business Area Information Model into run streams based on the geographical location of processes, the type of processing (batch or on-line), and the temporal requirements. Associate the transactions with their user interfaces (i.e., screens, reports, and manual procedures), and map them to the identified external transactions.

For the modules not translated in Business Area Analysis, determine the translation from the data flow diagrams in the Business Area Information Model to program modules. Using transform analysis and transaction analysis, translate the data flow diagram into a structure chart for each transaction run stream identified above. Determine the operational sequence of the identified modules, specify the sequence in which the modules must be performed, and group the modules according to this sequence. Finally, examine the charts for module cohesion, coupling, and design heuristics.

Determine Application Software Logic

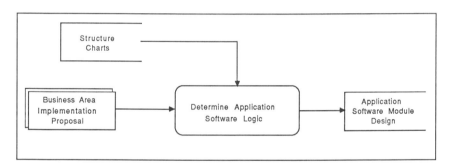

The purpose of this task is to translate the policy specifications from the Business Area Information Model into application logic modules. To accomplish this, create an action diagram for each structure chart developed in the previous task. Also verify the action diagrams developed from the processes on the data flow diagrams in Business Area Analysis.

Add physical specifications to the action diagrams (such as name, number, interface parameters, and implementation method), and modify the action diagrams. Identify any existing modules reusable in this application. These modules include program skeleton products (e.g., file update and screen processing) and commonly used routines (e.g., check digit routines). In GAMMA, copy these products, assigning new names and modifying their Narrative, General Information, and Note panels.

Identify standardized procedural steps (e.g., calculations) that are used throughout the activity model and for which there are no existing reusable modules. Specify the logic for these modules. In GAMMA, create program or Substitution Group products for each of these modules by specifying the logic within the Narrative panels. For the remaining modules, document detail logic from process descriptions in the activity model. Document the logic within the Narrative panels.

Develop Distributed Processing Design

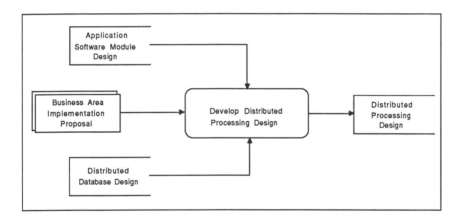

The processing design for a distributed system is developed in this task. To develop this design, identify the locations that the distributed system will encompass; identify the software modules (i.e., functions) required at each location; and group the modules, depending on location. If necessary, coordinate these activities with the database specialist.

Develop Critical Success Factors Map

To establish the traceability of strategy and policy to the associated software components, it is necessary to develop a Critical Success Factor Map. Determine the associations between the Critical Success Factors and the application software module design. Identify and map each Crit-

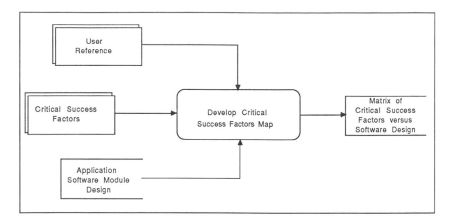

ical Success Factor related to a Business Area to the associated external design element that supports the Critical Success Factor. Map the external design element to the associated internal transactions developed in the "Develop Modules and Module Interfaces" task.

Package Detail System Design

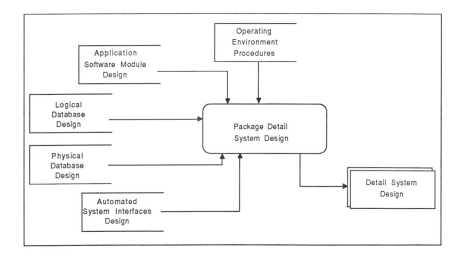

In this task, the Detail System Design components are organized for formal review and approval. Assemble the following:

Operating Environment Procedures
Application Software Module Design

Automated System Interfaces Design

Database Structure Design

Physical Database Design.

This task is not necessary in GAMMA, since packaging occurs automatically via the Design Manual.

DESIGN CONVERSION SYSTEM

This activity serves to verify the procedural and resource requirements for loading the database of the new system from both manual and automated sources of data. It also serves to specify the software, training materials, and operational procedures needed to guide the construction of the conversion system.

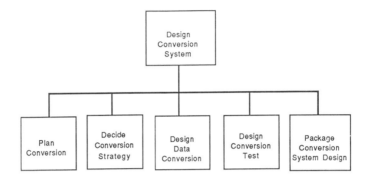

Plan Conversion

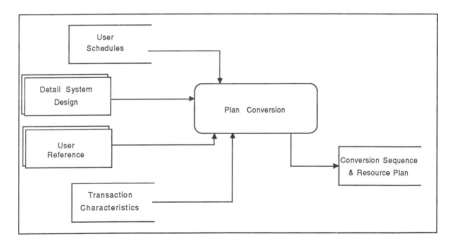

This task is performed to document the sequence and the resources required to accomplish the conversion. To determine the conversion sequence, sketch a rough conversion sequence based on the requirements from Business Area Analysis and System Design tasks. Then define the sequence of steps that will be performed to load the database and to verify that it is correct. Meet with user management to complete the conversion sequence and to assign individuals to steps for which users are responsible. Finally, document the conversion sequence and responsibilities, and review the conversion sequence with the project team and with user management.

After determining the conversion sequence, prepare initial estimates of the people and computer resources required for each conversion step. Determine approximately when resources will be required, based on a review of the workpapers from the "Determine Transaction Characteristics" task. Review user-controlled resource requirements with user management to determine if they conflict with business requirements and to resolve any conflicts. Also review the information-system-controlled resource requirements to determine possible conflicts, and resolve them, if necessary.

Develop the schedule for the conversion and document the conversion resources and schedule. Also develop the schedule for the change-over to the new system in the production mode.

Decide Conversion Strategy

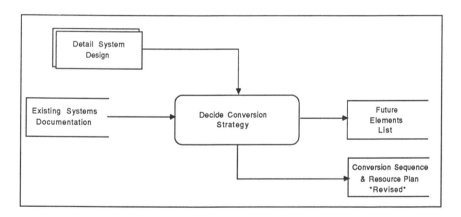

The purpose of this task is to document the source for each element in the new database and to understand the conversion at the lowest level of detail. For each element in the physical schema, determine the source, if any, in the current system. Determine the functions required to convert current data into the future schema format. Review and refine conversion rules with user management; divide the conversion into manual and automated steps; and revise the conversion sequence based on the detailed information collected in this task. Finally, review the conversion with the project team to determine if any additional edits are required by the new system.

Design Data Conversion

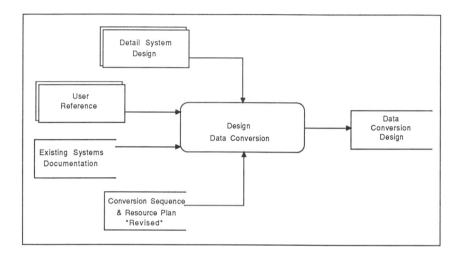

Specifications and procedures must be developed to convert data from existing systems to the future system. Begin by dividing the automated steps of the conversion sequence into program units.

Design the software required to load the manually prepared data into formatted files. (If GAMMA is used, its "Data Element" and "Product Where Used" lists will aid in this task.) Prototype the entry of manual data, and review for possible use the application prototypes developed in the "Prototype User Interfaces" task. Define additional screens to allow for manual data entry and for checking the completeness and quality of the data entered. Collect sample documents so that they can be reviewed for completeness and entered into the conversion data entry system. (In GAMMA, use the prototype feature in the Execute Functions Sub-Menu to simulate conversion entry.)

Reestimate resource requirements for the conversion, based on more detailed information, and update the appropriate GAMMA documentary product. Revise the conversion sequence if appropriate.

Design the conversion software for automated data, defining specifications for all of the programs that convert existing automated files and the newly loaded files of manual data into the future physical files. If GAMMA is used, create initial program products by defining their specifications in the Narrative panels for each program product that will convert an existing automated file.

Package the lists of data elements mapped from current to future in the "Decide Conversion Strategy" task. From this list of elements, take the portion that relates to automated file conversion and match the data to their associated program (i.e., the program that will convert the data to their new format). Collect a sample printout of conversion data sources and verify that the data match the published layouts. Develop conversion procedures for unrecoverable data errors, error handling, missing data, and data correction.

Finally, identify the steps in the conversion sequences that are complicated enough to warrant additional manual procedures. These steps might include manual data-entry steps requiring some input preparation tasks before key-entry. Batch balancing of control totals might also be included.

Design Conversion Test

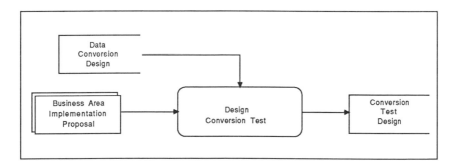

The purpose of this task is to develop the sequence of tests and acceptance criteria that will be used to verify a successful conversion. Define and document conversion acceptance test criteria. For each testing step, note the quantity of items that will be tested, and also specify the level of accuracy required.

To design the conversion tests, sketch a test sequence and detail the sequence of tests that will be performed to verify the conversion. Meet with user management to expand the sequence of tests, and revise sequence of conversion to include testing steps.

Package Conversion System Design

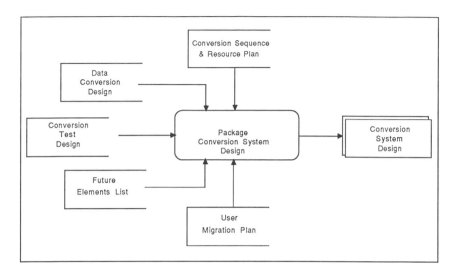

Organize the conversion design task outputs for formal review and approval by assembling the following:

Conversion Sequence and Resource Plan

Future Elements List

Data Conversion Design

Conversion Test Design

User Migration Plan.

Distribute these documents, conduct appropriate reviews, and revise them as required.

DESIGN SYSTEM TESTS

The purpose of this activity is to develop test plans and procedures, to define the test environment, and to specify the test data, scenarios, and software required to verify that the system performs as it should.

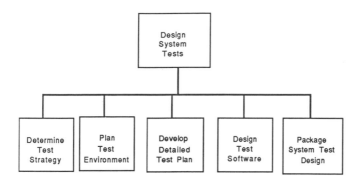

Determine Test Strategy

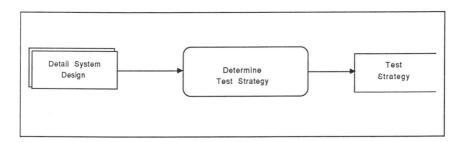

To establish the user and system test strategy, which will later serve to form the basis for a detailed test plan, determine the tests that are appropriate for the specific system. Use the matrix of recommended tests in Exhibit A at the end of this chapter. Develop test scripts that detail the testing steps required within each of the tests, and review the strategy with user management.

One strategy that may be used is to sequence the testing steps so that systems which produce data for other systems are tested first. If this is possible, verify that the construction sequence matches the testing sequence so that modules will be ready when needed. The implementation strategy may also have an impact here; that is, if the system is to be phased in one subsystem at a time, testing sequences should reflect this.

Plan Test Environment

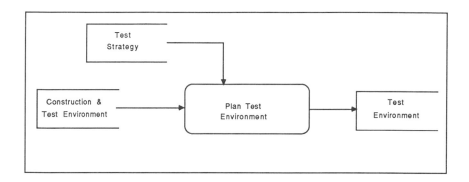

Plan the test environment by identifying the resources needed to support the testing process. Begin by determining what software is available on site and in the marketplace. (Note that GAMMA interfaces with the CA-DATAMACS Test Data Generator.) Meet with information systems management to specify the tools to be used and to discuss the benefits and costs of acquiring tools not already owned.

Determine any required test tools that are not already available for the project, and determine alternatives in the event that additional tools cannot be acquired or do not work as planned. Also determine the testing libraries that are needed for programs (source and object) and for data (execution/job control). Consult existing data center procedures for testing library conventions. One set of test libraries for each test stage (e.g., wait, integration, and system) may be appropriate. In GAMMA, document the results of this task as a documentary product.

Develop Detailed Test Plan

The purpose of this task is to develop a detailed test plan that supports the test strategy, defined in the "Determine Test Strategy" task, within the planned test environment developed in the "Plan Test Environment" task. Begin by creating detailed test scripts. For each, list the groups of test cases and their sequence. For each test group, list the characteristics for each test case.

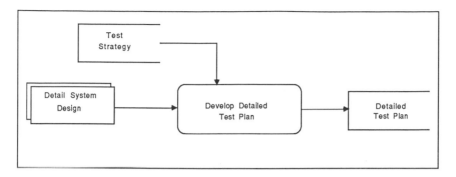

Meet with user management to determine which tests constitute the user acceptance test. Determine and document the assumptions concerning test activities, and determine the procedures for testing. Develop procedures for conducting tests. These procedures should cover coordination with the development team for updates; retesting after updates are performed; the coordination and use of the test libraries; and collecting statistics for project management and performance tuning. In GAMMA, document the results of this task as a documentary product.

Design Test Software

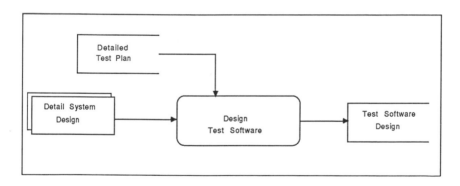

Design the custom software tools required to support testing activities. To do this, identify the custom software needed for testing as determined in the "Plan Test Environment" task. Define specifications for any testing drivers that are needed. In GAMMA, create initial program products for test drivers by documenting specifications in the GAMMA

Narrative panels. Finally, define specifications for any software that will be used to track problems and their resolution.

Package System Test Design

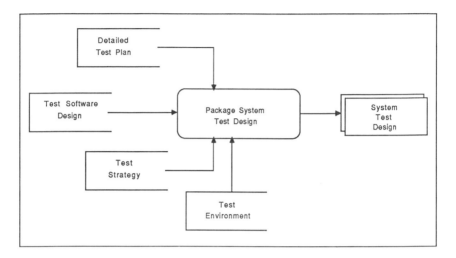

Organize the System Test Design task outputs for formal review and approval by assembling the following:

Test Strategy
Test Environment
Detailed Test Plan
Test Software Design.

After distributing these documents, review them with user management and revise them as required.

DESIGN TRAINING PROGRAM

Training programs must be designed to provide users, operators, the conversion team, and the maintenance team with the knowledge and skills they will need to perform their respective functions successfully.

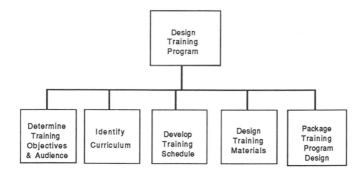

Determine Training Objectives and Audience

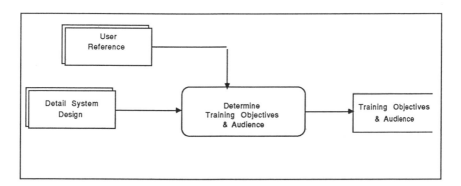

Establish the scope of the training program by identifying with user management the audience requiring training; identifying the needed skills and methods that change, from the user's view; and identifying the objectives for training.

Identify Curriculum

The purpose of this task is to define the required training sessions. To accomplish this, determine the learning strategy and the training sessions that will be needed. Group training ojectives by subject mat-

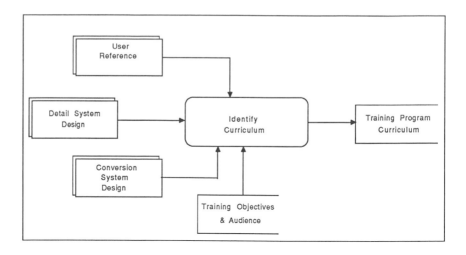

ter and skills, and develop a subject matter outline. Also determine environmental requirements and identify facilities, presentation media, and computer hardware and software.

Develop Training Schedule

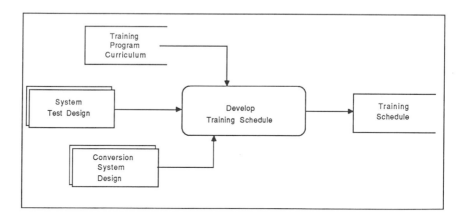

To establish the overall sequence and timing for training delivery, determine the timing for each group's first use of the new system for testing, data conversion, and system operation. Prepare a preliminary schedule such that the required training for each group is completed in time for assistance in conversion or for the first use of the operational system.

Design Training Materials

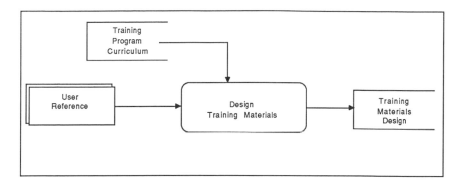

The purpose of this task is to provide designs for constructing training materials. For each topic in the subject matter outline developed earlier, list appropriate training materials. Identify materials that already exist and materials that can be produced by other system development activities. Design the format, content, and media for the remaining materials.

Package Training Program Design

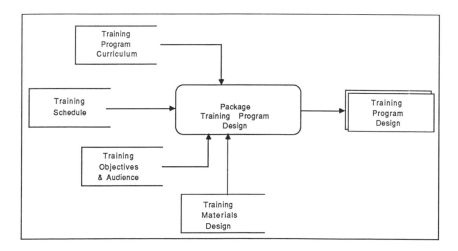

Organize the training program design task outputs for formal review by assembling the following:

Training Objectives and Audience
Training Program Curriculum
Training Schedule
Training Materials Design.

PERFORM PROJECT APPROVAL AND ASSESSMENT TASKS

To perform the approval and assessment tasks required to complete the System Design phase project, obtain approvals for phase deliverables and assess the performance of project team members.

EXHIBIT A

Test	Application Objective	Code Generator	Package Software	Custom Software
Crash Test	Verify a program handles one or two transactions without crashing.	x		x
Unit Test	Verify a program handles all transaction types appropriately.	x	x	x
Integration Test	Verify the system accepts input from or provides output to other systems with which it interfaces.	x	x	x
	For Maintenance Changes			
Regression Test	Verify the system handles sequences of transactions correctly throughout.	x	x	x
Volume Test	Verify the system can process the volume of transactions expected. Use simulation or actual data entry for tests.	x	x	x
Acceptance Test	User verifies the system is ready for production.	x	x	x

SYSTEM DESIGN PHASE DELIVERABLES

I. Detail System Design
   A. Operating Environment Procedures
   B. Application Software Module Design
   C. Automated System Interfaces Design
   D. Database Structure Design
   E. Physical Database Design
   F. Database Schema/Subschema Definitions
II. User Reference
   A. User Interface Prototypes
   B. Manual Procedures
   C. Package Interface Design
   D. User Transactions
   Appendix (For User Management Only)
       Organizational Changes
       User Migration Plan
III. Conversion System Design
   A. Conversion Sequence and Resource Plan
   B. Future Elements List
   C. Data Conversion Design
   D. Conversion Test Design
   E. User Migration Plan
IV. System Test Design
   A. Test Strategy
   B. Test Environment
   C. Detailed Test Plan
   D. Test Software Design
V. Training Program Design
   A. Training Objectives and Audience
   B. Training Program Curriculum
   C. Training Schedule
   D. Training Materials Design

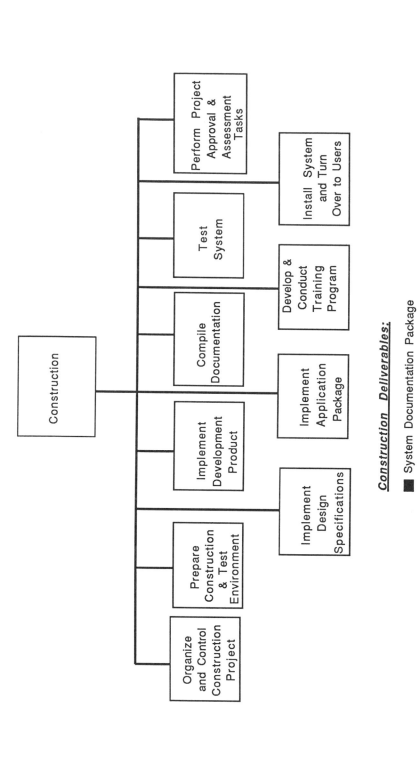

Construction

- Organize and Control Construction Project
- Prepare Construction & Test Environment
    - Implement Design Specifications
- Implement Development Product
    - Implement Application Package
- Compile Documentation
    - Develop & Conduct Training Program
- Test System
    - Install System and Turn Over to Users
- Perform Project Approval & Assessment Tasks

Construction Deliverables:

- ■ System Documentation Package
- ■ Operational Database
- ■ Installed Operational System
- ■ System Operating Procedures
- ■ Training Program

6

CONSTRUCTION PHASE

Construction is the fourth phase of the Information Engineering process. The objectives of this phase are to build and implement the system defined in the System Design phase, to develop effective procedures for operating the system, and to train users to operate the system effectively.

The development of rigorous analysis and design products during previous Information Engineering phases should result in smooth, controlled and rapid progress during Construction.

Goals

Construct and install a system that conforms to the design specifications.

Provide a high-quality system, from the user's perspective.

Meet the guidelines of the enterprise for system auditability, security, and data archiving.

Develop procedures for the day-to-day operation and maintenance of the system.

Develop a training program for operators and users, and conduct training.

Approach

This Guide describes the steps for implementing two types of specification:

Specifications for implementing a development product from an internal design specification. This design specification may employ a code generator such as GAMMA.

Specifications for implementing selected application packages.

Activities common to both implementations are outlined. These include training, system testing, production of final system documentation, and installation of the system in its production environment.

The use of prototypes and code generation are also outlined; the prototype may be used as a design specification for coding. The conversion of the prototype from specification to operational software is discussed, and the use of a code generator is illustrated through a discussion of GAMMA and how it is applied in the Construction phase.

Deliverables

System Documentation Package

Training Program

System Operating Procedures

Operational Database

Installed Operational System

Considerations

Information Engineering places emphasis on analysis and design. Therefore the Construction phase should begin with complete, detailed, and accurate specifications that can be coded directly into automated functions. If GAMMA is used by the project team, these specifications may be supplemented by partially completed programming products. Many of these may be in nearly finished form due to the prototyping activities of the last phase. The documentary products of GAMMA can be used throughout this phase as a workpaper repository for recording task work products.

Construction phase activities are organized by the type of activity to be performed, rather than by a sequential series of products to be created. For example, all testing tasks are described under the function "Test System," but the sequence in which they are performed may vary depending on the specific circumstances encountered.

The use of a code generator like GAMMA may result in some parts of the Construction phase overlapping System Design or even Business Area Analysis. For example, the building of prototypes, the conversion of data, the construction of training materials and their delivery, and the preparation of the construction and test environment may take place earlier in the production cycle.

ORGANIZE AND CONTROL CONSTRUCTION PROJECT

The Construction phase requires close attention to task completion. Varied technical skills are required. As the project team grows, coordinating the activities of team members and managing interdependencies become critical to timely task completion. The management tasks for Construction continue the same set of tasks identified in System Design, but the greater precision of the work products requires stricter management.

To initiate and manage the project, perform the following tasks:

Organize and train the project team;

Develop and revise the work unit plan;

Review actual versus planned activities;

Review work products;

Analyze the consistency of project definitions and the proposed design;

Evaluate change requests;

Review and revise control procedures;

Report on project status;

Perform short-interval scheduling.

PREPARE CONSTRUCTION AND TEST ENVIRONMENT

This activity is composed of a series of tasks that must be performed to establish the hardware and software environments in order for remaining Construction activities to proceed. If prototyping is used to uncover requirements, this activity may be performed as early in the development cycle as Business Area Analysis.

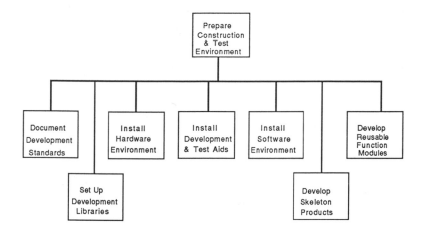

Document Development Standards

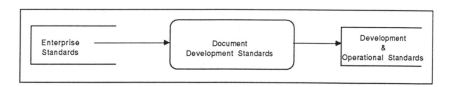

Document development standards by identifying and revising any existing standards for software development projects. If none exist, establish standards. To identify existing standards, survey information systems management to obtain the organization's standards for:

Programming conventions

User interfaces (e.g., screen conventions and sign-on procedures)

Help interfaces

System conventions

Naming conventions

Construction procedures

Library standards for migration controls

Testing standards and procedures.

When GAMMA is used on the project, identify the need for standardized report and screen headings and create Substitution Group products for these. Document the completion of this task and the source for development standards. New standards should be recorded in a GAMMA documentary product. When using a code generator, installation standards (such as file and data element naming) may require modification.

Set up Development Libraries

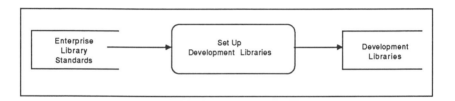

The purpose of this task is to determine and set up the required automated libraries to be shared by the development team. If necessary, create the identified libraries, including the required authorization, access, and security controls. Necessary test, integration, and production libraries include those for source code, object code, execution control, job control, and documentation.

Install Hardware Environment

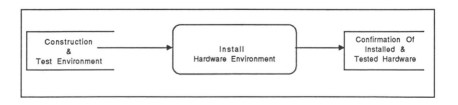

Arrange for the installation of the hardware required for the new system, as defined in the System Design task "Define Construction and Test Environment." Coordinate with information systems management to have hardware for the data center, distributed systems, and/or networks installed. After the installation has been completed, confirm that a test of the system hardware has also been successfully completed.

Install Development and Test Aids

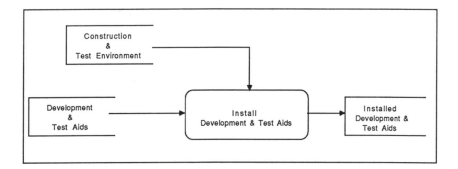

Arrange for the installation of the necessary software to allow construction and testing to proceed (as defined in the System Design task "Define Construction and Test Environment"). Identify the necessary software to aid in the development and testing of the new system. These software tools include:

Interactive Debuggers

Database Utilities

Screen Painters

Code Generators (e.g., GAMMA)

Dump Formatters/Analyzers

Test Utilities and Test Data Generators

Network Debugging Utilities

Satellite/Personal Computer Compilers.

Coordinate with systems programming administration for the installation and testing of the software aids to be used.

Install Software Environment

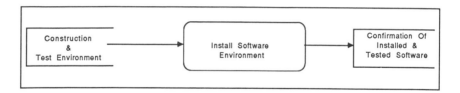

The purpose of this task is to install the operating-system software required for execution of the new system, as defined in the System Design task "Define Construction and Test Environment." Coordinate and/or confirm the successful installation or existence of the system software with the Database Administrator or Systems Programmer. Ensure that the new system is defined or listed on any relevant tables of the system software. Coordinate with the Database Administrator or Systems Programmer to ensure the new system definitions are defined in the system generations.

Develop Skeleton Products

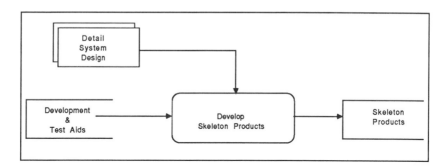

Skeleton products, such as source copy members, are built to provide a collection of generic framework products that can be used to speed up the development process. In a COBOL environment, these would take the form of generic Data Descriptions (record descriptions), Working Storage Definitions, Linkage Sections, and Format Statements. These are included in the source copy library with any other code that will be used more than once in the system.

Skeleton products include generic program types (such as transaction processor, database access, and screen maps); compile, link, and run procedures; test harnesses; and diagnostic routines. These skeleton products and source copy members may be obtained from previously designed reusable assets. In certain environments, the team will also need to complete the procedural logic panels for new program products here.

Develop Reusable Function Modules

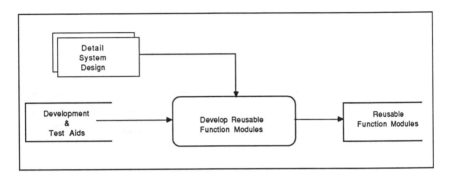

The purpose of this task is to identify and build a set of reusable modules that are shared during the development process. To accomplish this, identify and build commonly used functions in the system design (e.g., updates to both an employee file and a benefits file when new employee is added). Document the function modules, and make them available to the development team.

In GAMMA, complete the procedural logic for each reusable module. For modules defined as Substitution Group products, complete the variable symbol definitions and the detail substitution logic. For reusable modules other than Substitution Groups, complete the procedural logic panels.

IMPLEMENT DESIGN SPECIFICATIONS

Once the hardware and software environments have been established,
the team is ready to begin transforming the System Design specifications, including any prototypes, into automated working units of the
system.

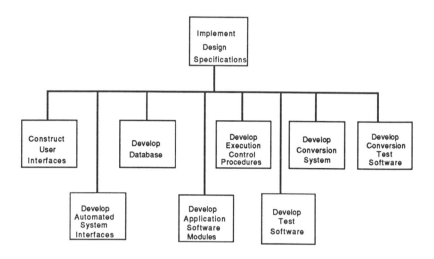

Construct User Interfaces

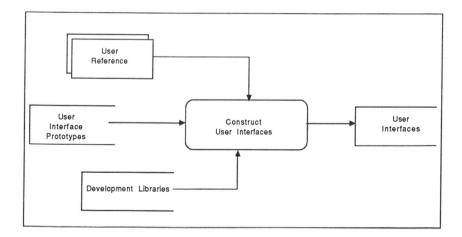

In this task, the objective is to build a consistent, high-quality user interface for the new system. This interface must be coordinated with the installed package interface if an application package is being used.

To begin, construct the screens, using the prototypes developed in the System Design phase as a base. If edit checking was not completed in the prototype base, edit checks should be included.

In GAMMA, complete any required procedural logic panels for previously developed screen prototypes and invoke Substitution Groups, created earlier, for standardized headings. Build the screen/transaction links, taking into consideration communication and switching between transactions and the design of transaction backout. Also construct the Report Layouts, construct the on-line help system and the on-line user manual (if specified in the design workpapers), and develop the system control interface.

Develop Automated System Interfaces

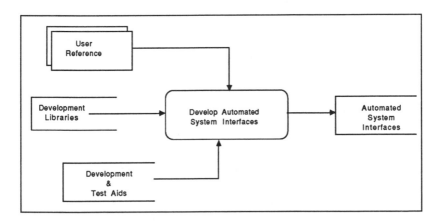

The purpose of this task is to construct the interfaces that acquire data and transfer data between automated systems and the new system, as defined in the User Reference. To do this, code the logic modules, compile and link them, and verify they can interact with the data structures of the other system(s).

If using GAMMA, complete all programming products that relate to automated system interfaces. The procedural logic panels are completed to finish building each product. Also coordinate with the network specialist, if the interface will involve a communications network.

Develop Database

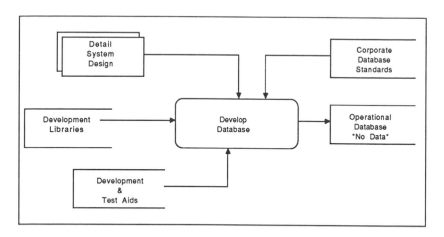

During this task, construct an operational database for the new system, as defined in the Detail System Design. To complete this task:

Refine the database schema definition, if required.

Ensure the accuracy of the record structures, field attributes, indexes, and or relational views for the chosen Database Management System.

Modify the appropriate database products, if revisions affect the logical or physical data structures (e.g., layout or blocksize).

Verify the system parameters needed to generate the database schema definition.

Generate the definition.

Allocate the storage space for the database.

Place the database storage structure on the storage device.

Initialize the database.

Develop Application Software Modules

To develop the application software modules as designed in the Detail System Design, code the modules exactly from the design speci-

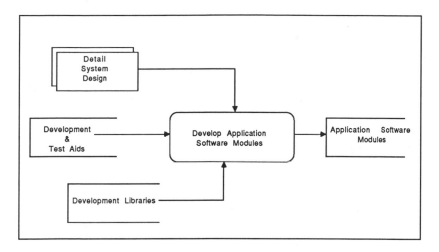

fications. No additional design work should be required. Compile the software programs, and link the programs into the system development library.

When GAMMA is used, generate the system by completing the System Control Card panel to select processor run options, completing the Job Submittal panels to create a batch job run stream for generating code, and link-editing the generated code into the system development library.

Develop Execution Control Procedures

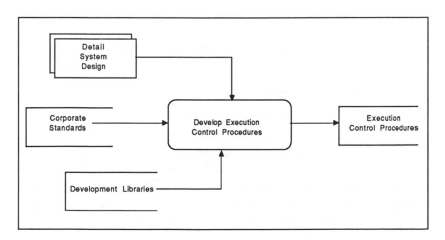

In this task, develop the command or control language procedures necessary for programs to operate in the system environment, (such as Job Control Language or Command Procedures). In GAMMA, the Job Control section of the Design Manual will aid in completing this task. The job control statements generated can be customized to specific installation standards.

Develop Test Software

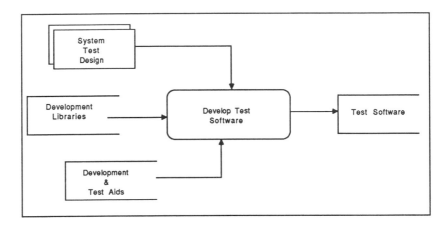

To develop the custom test software required to support the testing activities as described in the System Test Design, code the software modules from design specifications (Test Software Design). In GAMMA, complete the programming products by coding the procedural logic for each product, and generate source code. Finally, compile the software programs and link them into the system test library.

Develop Conversion System

A subsystem is constructed to convert existing data to the new system, as defined in the System Design activity "Design Conversion System." This may involve developing a large number of complex modules. Develop the software modules from the specifications generated in the System Design task "Design Data Conversion." In GAMMA, complete the programming products by coding the procedural logic for each product, generate source code, and link the conversion programs, using the system conversion library.

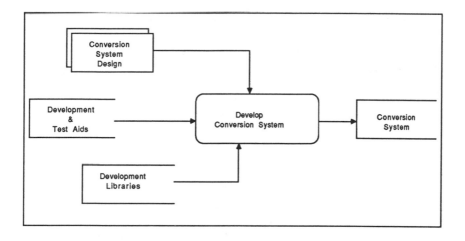

Develop Conversion Test Software

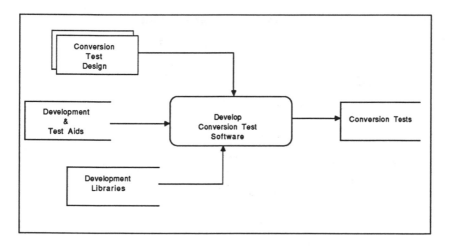

The purpose of this task is to construct the test software required to validate the data conversion from existing systems to the new system as described in the System Design task "Design Conversion Test."

This is accomplished by developing the conversion test from the specifications in the Conversion Test Design, and by completing the programming products for the Conversion Test Design and generating source code.

Also compile the test programs and link the programs into the system test library.

IMPLEMENT DEVELOPMENT PRODUCT

In this activity, the Construction team prepares a functional system ready to be installed into the production environment.

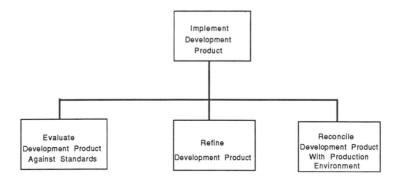

Evaluate Development Product Against Standards

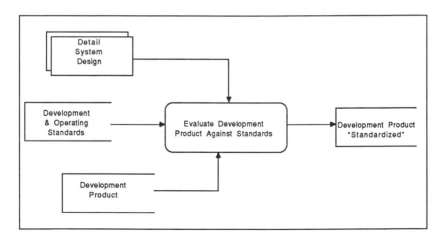

This task is conducted to ensure that the development product conforms to the organization's development and operational standards. Compare the application software modules against the documented development and operational standards, and make all necessary changes to the system to ensure conformity. If using a code generator, this task may be omitted.

Refine Development Product

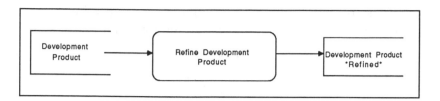

The purpose of this task is to revise the development product to increase its efficiency and maintainability. Review the development product to identify and repair inefficiencies and poorly written code (coordinated with performance testing), and expand functions as required. This task may not be necessary when using a code generator, since it generates efficient, well structured source code. A review should be made of procedural code written by the team to identify inefficiencies and areas in need of expanded function.

Reconcile Development Product with Production Environment

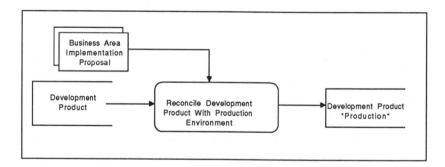

The development product is revised as necessary so that it will function in the production environment. To do this, identify any differences in the production environment that will affect the development product, (e.g., the Job Control Language may require changes if moved from the development machine to the production environment). Revise the development product to reconcile these differences.

IMPLEMENT APPLICATION PACKAGE

The purpose of this activity is to install a commercial software application package and to develop the package interfaces for the new system.

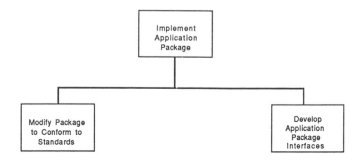

Modify Package to Conform to Standards

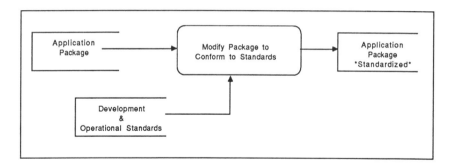

To modify the package to meet the operating standards established by the information systems organization, compare the package with documented development and operating standards. Make all necessary changes to ensure conformity.

Develop Application Package Interfaces

The purpose of this task is to develop and implement the package interfaces to the development product, as defined in the User Reference. In completing this task, program the identified interfaces to connect the selected package with the external design of the new system. Complete

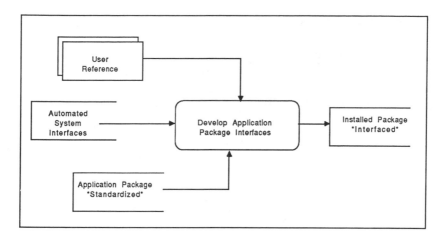

the programming products for the application package interfaces, compile and link the interface program modules, and install the package. Also, verify that the interfaces (e.g., screens) of the application package to the external design of the new system function as expected.

COMPILE DOCUMENTATION

Documentation is compiled to provide a reference for enterprise management, system developers, system users, and auditors, and to increase the enterprise knowledge base for future planning (Librarian Function). If GAMMA has been used throughout the System Design and Construction phases, much of this documentation can be obtained from the GAMMA Design Manual.

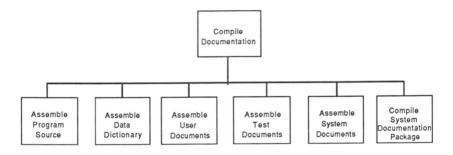

Assemble Program Source

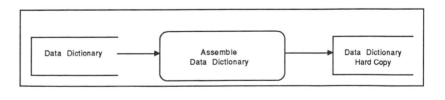

Program sources are assembled to provide a hard copy representation of program code and comments. Gather and organize the hard copy of compiled source code, including the compilation maps, depending upon particular system utilities.

Assemble Data Dictionary

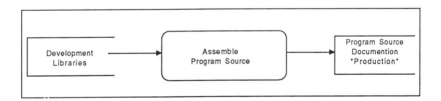

The purpose of this task is to provide a common description, usage, and understanding of the components of the implemented system. Generate a hard copy of the database data dictionary, dependent upon the particular DBMS technology used in building the system.

Assemble User Documents

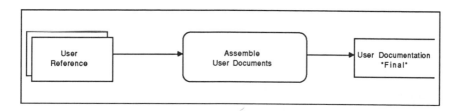

User documents are assembled to provide a complete set of instructions for using and maintaining the system. Refine the User Reference created during the System Design phase to match the actual system operation. This work product can be obtained from GAMMA's Design Manual.

Assemble Test Documents

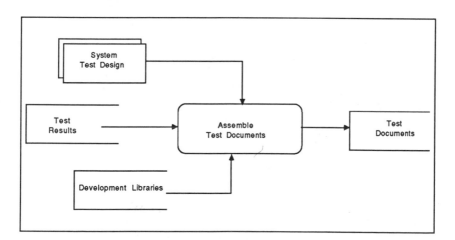

The purpose of this task is to assemble test documents to maintain an organized, reviewable collection of test procedures and results. Test documents should be maintained to a degree where tests can be reexecuted during maintenance. These documents should include:

Inventory of Tested Data
Test Data
Test Cases and Descriptions
Test Plan
Test Scripts
Output Report Mockups
Screen Display Mockups
Predicted and Actual Results.

These work products can be obtained from GAMMA's Design Manual.

Assemble System Documents

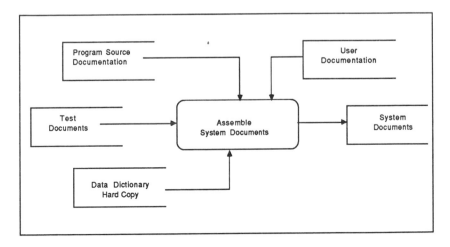

System documents are assembled to provide reference material for system builders and maintainers so that problems and changes to the system can be handled in a quick and orderly fashion with minimal effect on production. Organize the documents developed during previous phases of this project. This work product can also be obtained from GAMMA's Design Manual.

Compile System Documentation Package

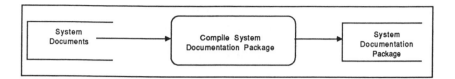

The purpose of this task is to organize the project documentation for formal review and approval. In carrying out this task, package program source documentation, data dictionary hardcopy, user documentation, test documents, and system documents.

DEVELOP AND CONDUCT TRAINING PROGRAM

The objective of this activity is to provide a detailed program to train selected personnel to use and maintain the implemented system.

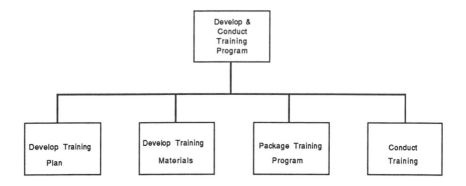

Develop Training Plan

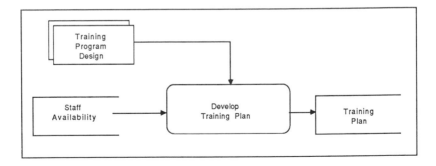

Develop a final plan for training users, operators, and the conversion team. The plan should allow for appropriate scheduling of people, resources, and materials. Using the design of the training schedule as defined in the Training Program Design, document any undeveloped training materials (as well as who will be developing them), the time and location of training, who will be receiving the training, and who will be conducting the training.

Develop Training Materials

The purpose of this task is to develop a final set of materials that will enable system users to operate the new system effectively. Begin

by organizing training materials that were produced by other systems building activities, including the System Design task "Design Training Materials." Then develop an "Instructor Guide" for each course, covering the subject matter as outlined in the Training Program Design.

If using GAMMA, document the completion of this task in a GAMMA documentary product.

Package Training Program

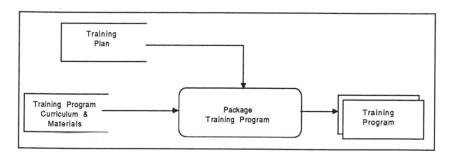

In this task, organize the training program for implementation, review, and user reference. The assembled training program documents should cover a training plan and training program curricula and materials. Determine the packaging procedures, collect the work products, and review these with user management.

Conduct Training

Training is conducted to allow users to gain knowledge and experience with the implemented system in a structured setting. Prepare for the training sessions (organize the classroom, set up terminals, reproduce materials). Conduct the training sessions, providing training for personnel at the appropriate time according to the schedule. This training

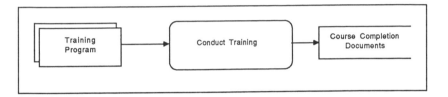

could be for users, both management and clerical, for the conversion team, or for the operators of the new system. Evaluate the success of training to determine if user understanding of the new system meets the objectives. Schedule additional training sessions if required.

TEST SYSTEM

The system must be tested to ensure that all development products function properly and conform to specifications as defined in the System Test Design. The exact order of testing will vary depending on circumstances. For example, the integration test and the performance test may be performed periodically as more modules are added to the system, while crash tests and unit tests are typically performed once, immediately after product completion. When using GAMMA, the completion of the various testing tasks should be recorded in a documentary product as they are finished.

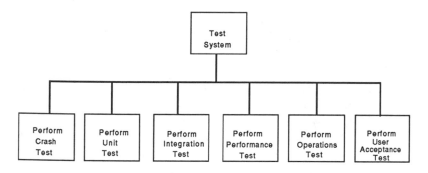

Perform Crash Test

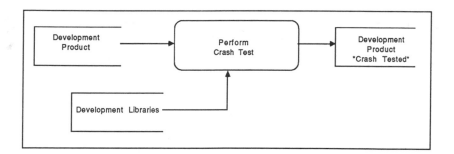

A crash test is conducted to determine the completion of the coding task. Execute the crash test to exercise the development product. This test, conducted by the module developer, proves that the module meets the minimal requirements—a functional component which accepts defined input and generates defined output. Review the results, making any revisions necessary, and continue testing until errors have been corrected.

Perform Unit Test

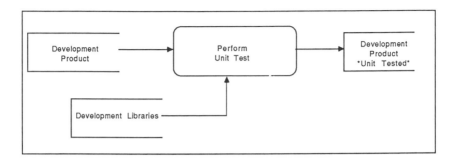

The unit test ensures that the product under development conforms to specifications and handles all normal and exception cases properly. Execute the unit test to exercise the development product using the test case identified during design. This test, conducted by the module developer, also ensures that the interfaces that integrate the modules are tested. Review the results, making necessary revisions, and continue testing until errors have been corrected.

Perform Integration Test

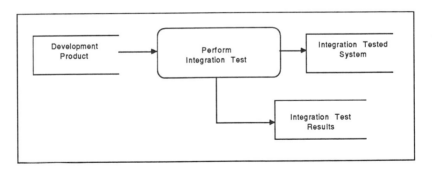

The integration test ensures that the product under development functions properly and conforms to specifications that integrate into a working group, either a subsystem or a complete system. Combine the development products into a group of products; and then execute the integration test plan developed during the System Design phase, measuring the compatibility of the new system with other systems. Review the results and make necessary revisions. A separate test team may be responsible for integration testing, but when problems are identified, the module is sent back to the developer.

Perform Performance Test

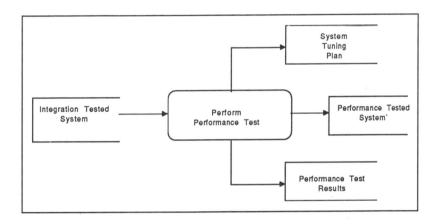

The performance test ensures that the new system meets performance requirements under the specified range of work load conditions, including peak periods and other stress conditions. Execute the performance test plan developed during the System Design phase. During volume testing, measure throughput, response time, and resource use.

Analyze variances and review the results with user and information systems management. Failure to meet performance requirements may be resolved by reducing user demand, tuning the system software/hardware/communications environment, or reworking portions of the application. (The last alternative is extremely costly; if the possibility of performance constraints affecting system acceptance exists, resource consumptive portions of the system should be isolated and modeled prior to system design).

Perform Operations Test

The operations test ensures that the new system procedures perform properly in the production operations environment, and that the system operators are capable of dealing with them under normal conditions.

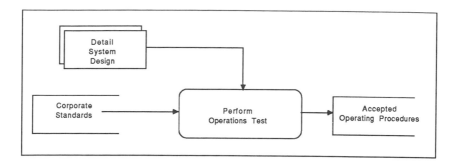

Turn over operation materials to the data center staff (or other individuals with responsibility for operating the system). Then arrange for the operations staff to execute the operating procedures of normal system startup and shutdown; archiving; backup and recovery; and restart after application failure, system software failure, and communication network failure. Review the results and make necessary revisions. In many cases, especially if new hardware/software or unusual procedures are being introduced, operator training should precede this task.

Perform User Acceptance Test

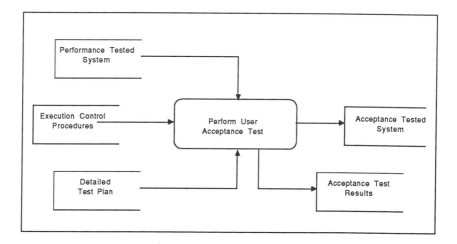

The user acceptance test ensures that the new system meets user management requirements. This task typically requires a good deal of preparation and support (such as hardware and software coordination, and release-level versions of the application linked and ready). Arrange for the user to execute the sequence of acceptance test cases developed (and approved by the user) in the System Design task entitled "Develop Detailed Test Plan." The tests should be executed using the loaded database.

Allow the user to operate the system freely in the test environment for an agreed-upon time period. Evaluate the acceptance test results and debrief the user for comments relating to system interface, system performance, and system functionality.

Fix any minor problems immediately, fix any failures to meet approved requirements, and submit change control requests for other major changes.

INSTALL SYSTEM AND TURN OVER TO USER

The next activity in the Construction phase is to install the new system, including the database, in its production environment. When using GAMMA, the completion of the various system installation tasks should be recorded in a documentary product.

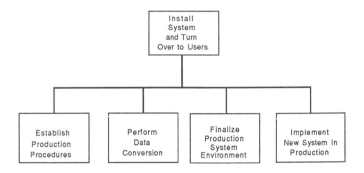

Establish Production Procedures

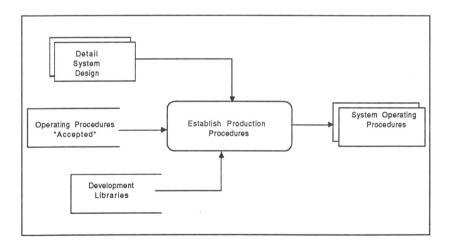

Production procedures are established to ensure that procedures to operate the new system are in place in the data center, or other environment where the production system will operate. Set up operating environment procedures, as defined in the Detail System Design. These procedures include normal system operation, restart/recovery, database maintenance, database backup, security and audit, and data conversion. Review the procedures with the data center personnel to ensure their understanding.

Perform Data Conversion

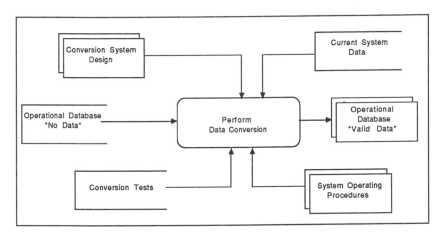

The purpose of this task is to load existing data into the new system's database, as defined in the Conversion System Design. Perform the data conversion procedures, which will execute the conversion system programs, and other database load utilities. Load manually prepared data into formatted files by entering the data into the conversion data entry system. Transform existing files and the newly loaded files of manual data into the new formats. Test the conversion by executing the conversion tests to verify data quality. Review the results to ensure the conversion acceptance test criteria are met.

Finalize Production System Environment

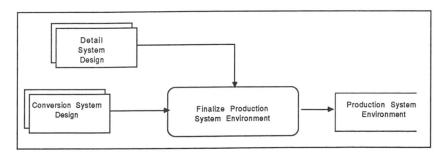

The team must arrange for the installation or enhancement of the production hardware and software environment necessary for the new system. During Construction, it is possible that the development team will be working in an environment that is smaller than the production system environment. If this is the case, it is necessary to install the new system using the expanded hardware and software.

Coordinate with systems programming administration to schedule the installation, install hardware and/or software, test, and tune the fully configured environment.

Coordinate with vendors to arrange for installation to meet the project schedule. Multiple product installations (that is, hardware, then system software, then a DBMS) require careful planning and testing at each stage.

Implement New System in Production

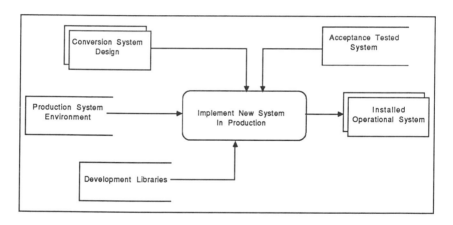

The purpose of this task is to implement the new system in the production environment. Move the new system to production mode according to the defined User Migration Plan in the Conversion System Design. The schedule and timing of the migration is outlined in the plan. Move the new programs to the production system library, coordinating with the Database Administrator or Systems Programmer to perform this function. Also move the new system components to the production libraries (e.g., Database Schema Definitions) and lock new system components in development and test libraries. A backup copy of the Internal Master File in GAMMA should be made and archived.

PERFORM PROJECT APPROVAL AND ASSESSMENT TASKS

The final activity in the Construction phase is to perform the approval and assessment tasks required to complete a Construction and installation phase project. The Construction team accomplishes this by obtaining approvals for phase deliverables, assessing performance, preparing the maintenance proposal, and preparing a post-installation review proposal.

CONSTRUCTION DELIVERABLES

  I. System Documentation Package
   - A. Program Source Documentation
   - B. Data Dictionary Hard Copy
   - C. User Documentation
   - D. Test Documents
   - E. System Documents

 II. Operational Database

III. Installed Operational System

IV. System Operating Procedures
   - A. Normal System Startup/Shutdown
   - B. Maintenance
   - C. Backup and Recovery
   - D. Security and Audit
   - E. Data Conversion

 V. Training Program
   - A. Training Plan
   - B. Instructor Guide
   - C. Student Materials
   - D. Curriculum
   - E. Course Schedule
   - F. Presentation Medium

GLOSSARY

Activity. Something an enterprise does to achieve a stated purpose. An activity can be a function or a process.

Activity model. A representation of a function or process.

Affinity analysis. A technique for identifying the degree of bonding between two objects.

Application package. A vendor-supplied automated system.

Association. A meaningful intersection between two objects (such as entities, processes, goals, or Critical Success Factors). Associations are used to capture intersection data.

Attribute. A type of characteristic or property describable in terms of a value possessed by entities of a given type.

Availability. The locations in the enterprise where information about its entities is required or modified. This information is classified by entity type or Subject Area.

"Best Guess" Clustering. A heuristic approach to defining Business Areas based on a consultant's industry knowledge and experience.

Business Area. A portion of an enterprise. A Business Area is defined by a set of highly cohesive processes and entities by using techniques such as clustering or factor analysis.

Business Area Analysis (BAA). A phase of Information Engineering; a set of work activities that identify and model data and activities needed to support a Business Area. During the Business Area Analysis phase, a Business Area Information Model, Business Area Requirements, a Business Area Technical Requirements

Report, an Enterprise Benefits Analysis, and a Business Area Implementation Proposal are produced.

Business Area Information Model. A product of a Business Area Analysis study. A Business Area Information Model is expressed via data and activity models and represents the processes and information needed within a Business Area by an enterprise.

Business Area project. A project to analyze a Business Area and produce a Business Area Information Model.

Business Function. A major, high-level activity of an enterprise; a collection of processes that together support one aspect of furthering the goals and Critical Success Factors of the enterprise.

Business plan. A high-level plan used by senior management to direct the enterprise. The plan should reference the information systems role within the organization and its expected contribution to enterprise strategies.

Cardinality. The number of instances of one type with respect to instances of another type.

Clustering. A technique for defining Business Areas by logically mapping entity types against functions or processes.

Construction. A phase of Information Engineering; a set of work activities that implement the application system design. The major products of the Construction phase are the System Documentation Package, a Training Program, System Operating Procedures, an Operational Data Base, and the Installed Operational System.

Corporate network strategy. A documented approach (based upon policies and procedures and their physical implementation) for creating the distribution links an enterprise requires to get the right information to the right people at the right time.

Critical Assumptions. A group of assumptions about the enterprise—and about its business environment, competition or industry—that supports or validates an enterprise's Critical Success Factors.

Critical Decisions. The decisions that must be made by an enterprise to actualize its Critical Success Factors.

Critical Information. The information that is required by an enterprise's operational systems to enable them to support the enterprise's Critical Success Factors.

Critical Success Factor (CSF). A result that is measurable and that will have a major influence on whether or not an organizational unit meets its objectives. An example of a Critical Success Factor is "acquire appropriate products to gain a market share."

Critical Success Factor Analysis. A process for extracting and reconciling Critical Success Factors.

Cultural changes. Changes in the enterprise's organizational structure, skill and staffing levels, job functions, or policies and procedures.

Data collection. A repository of data maintained by an enterprise, usually in the form of manual or electronic files. Also called a data store.

Data flow. A set of data flowing between two data nodes and representing facts about entities of interest to the enterprise.

Data flow diagram. A picture of the flows of data through a business activity or automated system; it shows the external agents that are sources or destinations of data, the activities that transform the data, and the places where the data are stored.

Data model. A diagram that represents the inherent properties of the data independent of the physical environment.

Data store. A logical data file.

Decomposition. A technique for partitioning an organization, activity, or Subject Area into its lower level components.

Decomposition Diagrammer. An Information Engineering Workbench tool used to draw decomposition diagrams, which are used to show the elements of a structure and their relationships.

Design Manual. A GAMMA feature for storing and organizing the systems documentation; portions of the Design Manual are used to control the application generation process.

Development product. A functional information system (custom software) installed in a production environment.

Distribution plan. A scheme for allocating an enterprise's processing and data across organizational units and locations. A distribution plan is used to implement all or part of a corporate network strategy.

Domain of automation. The portion of a Business Area that will be addressed by an application system.

Domain of change. The portions of a Current Business Area Information Model that change when creating the Future Business Area Information Model.

Encyclopedia. A central repository of knowledge relating to the enterprise and its goals, structure, strategies, functions, processes, procedures and systems.

Enterprise. An organization that exists to perform a mission and to achieve goals and objectives.

Enterprise Benefit Analysis. A cost-benefit analysis that takes both quantitative and qualitative information into account in assessing the impact of alternative domains of automation on both a Business Area and the enterprise.

Enterprise culture. The collective sense of traditions, conventions, and behavioral standards characteristic to a given enterprise, determined by organizational structure and by formal and informal human resources policies, procedures, and practices.

Enterprise Information Model. A description of the entity types, functions and processes that define an enterprise and of their interrelationships. Consists of an Enterprise Data Model, an Enterprise Activity Model, and an Enterprise Organization Model.

Entity type. A group of data describing a class of people, places, things, concepts, or events about which an enterprise stores information.

Entity-relationship diagram. A schematic that shows entity types and the associations between them, with cardinalities indicated.

Entity-relationship model. An entity-relationship diagram together with enterprise policy-based definitions of each entity type and relationship.

Event. A significant occurrence that triggers an activity or process and that must be recognized and reacted to by the system.

Event model. A diagram illustrating the valid states of a system and the transitions between states.

External agent. A data source or destination that is outside the scope of interest.

External event. A change in the external environment of the system under study. The system recognizes the change by a flow of data.

Factor analysis. A technique for defining Business Areas by using a statistical approach to uncover correlations between processes and entity types.

Functional representative. An operational specialist (typically, a line manager or designate) with expertise in a particular enterprise functional area. Used as an interview source during the Information Systems Planning and Business Area Analysis phases.

GAMMA. An application generator used during System Design and Construction.

Goal. An end or target state that is achieved by accomplishing all Critical Success Factors related to it.

Implementation Plan. A major product of Business Area Analysis; the Implementation Plan specifies the strategies to be used to design (optionally, to construct and install) the domain of automation for a Business Area.

Implementation Proposal. A Business Area Analysis phase product that defines design and construction strategies for the system being built.

Industry model. A generic Enterprise Information Model that is applicable to a range of enterprises within a given industry. Industry models are maintained (as templates awaiting customization) in the Information Engineering Workbench encyclopedia.

Information Engineer. An information systems professional who has been trained in and who practices Information Engineering.

Information Engineering. An interlocking set of formal techniques in which enterprise models, data models, and process models are built up in a comprehensive knowledge base and are used to create and maintain information systems.

Information Engineering Joint Application Design (IE-JAD). A strategy for rapid product development through end user and system professional participation in thorough, well structured group sessions under the control of a facilitator. Ideas are captured in computerized models via automated diagramming tools.

Information Engineering Workbench. An automated set of power tools for developing and maintaining the products of Information Engineering.

Information model. A high-level data model.

Information need. The information required by a particular person or organizational unit to make a decision or complete a task.

Information Needs Report. A major product of the Information Systems Planning phase; it contains the Executive Information Needs

Summary, functional Information Needs Summary, and Information Systems Needs Summary. The report is used to document the goals, Critical Success Factors, Critical Assumptions, problems, critical issues, strategies, and technical directions of an enterprise.

Information system. A system of data and processes that can be used to record and maintain information.

Information systems environment. The technologies, application portfolio, human resources, and management practices that constitute an enterprise's information systems capability.

Information Systems Group. A generic name for an enterprise's information systems organization.

Information Systems Plan. An Information Systems Planning phase deliverable, typically consisting of a set of priortized project definitions, a Tactical Information Systems Plan, a Long-Range Information Systems Plan, and a set of Plan Review Guidelines.

Information Systems Planning (ISP). A phase of Information Engineering; a high-level study of an enterprise (or of a portion of one) that identifies informaion needs, assesses existing information systems capabilities, and defines Business Areas. An Enterprise Information Model, Information Needs Report, Existing Information Systems Profile Report and Information Systems Plan (which includes a Tactical Information Systems Plan and a Long-Range Information Systems Plan) are produced.

Information Technology Plans. Inputs to an Information Systems Planning phase; these plans document information systems strategies and directions for an enterprise. Topics would include hardware and software, communications (voice and data), management policies and practices, and organizational issues.

Infrastructure project. A non-application-specific information systems project defined during Information Systems Planning and needed to support the enterprise.

Knowledge base. A data repository that contains information and knowledge about applying this information within a particular context.

Knowledge Coordinator. The portion of the Information Engineering Workbench responsible for applying the rules of Information Engineering to ensure the consistency and correctness of any information that will be saved in the knowledge base.

Locations. Geographic places where processes are performed and/or data are recorded and maintained for an enterprise.

Long-Range Information Systems Plan. A two-to-five year plan that identifies information systems projects at a level meaningful to an enterprise's senior management and top information systems management.

Migration Plan. A user-oriented plan for realigning organizational units, job descriptions and staffing levels to mesh effectively with a new information system.

Model. A representation of some aspect of an enterprise. A model is stored in the encyclopedia.

Modeling source. A person, group or document that provides the information used to model some aspect of the enterprise.

Network specialist. A generic term for any voice or data communications professional.

Object. Anything that can be entered into the Information Engineering Workbench encyclopedia.

Organizational unit. An administrative subdivision of an enterprise, partitioned along human resource lines, that exists to perform one or more processes.

Parent. An object in a decomposition that is immediately above a specified object. An object in a decomposition that has at least one object below it.

Perspective. A user view of an enterprise or of a portion of one; it is obtained by considering multiple diagrams (such as decomposition view, data view, or process view diagrams).

Problem. An obstacle to achieving a goal or Critical Success Factor; a situation or issue that presents uncertainty, complication, complexity, or difficulty.

Process. A low-level activity that starts and stops and is repeatedly executed. Each execution of a process produces a specific kind of effect on entities or information about entities of specific types. Decomposing a function yields its component processes.

Process dependency diagram. A diagram that indicates the high-level interaction between activities or processes, generally reflecting large aggregates of data. It is similar to a data flow diagram but reflects a higher level of detail.

Project. A related group of work activities, organized under the direction of a project manager using a project plan, which when carried out will allow the project goal(s) to be achieved. Examples are Business Area Analysis projects, infrastructure projects, and design projects.

Prototype. A working model; typically, a model that simulates system externals.

Prototyping. A strategy for communicating requirements and constraints through the development and exercising of a working model.

Relationship. A named connection or association between one or more entities that embodies some relevant information value for an enterprise.

Stakeholder. A key member of an organizational unit who defines and has a personal stake in achieving the goals of the unit.

State. The condition of a system at a point in time. Information about the state of a system, together with new events, determines the system's response.

Subject Area. A major, high-level classification of data; a group of entity types that pertain directly to a function or major topic of interest to the enterprise.

System Design. A phase of Information Engineering; Business Area requirements and models are used to develop detailed information system specifications. The major products of System Design are a User Reference, a System Test Design, a Conversion System Design, a Training Program Design, and a Detail System Design Report.

Tactical Information Systems Plan. A short-term information systems road map that specifies projects up to a two-year time horizon.

Technical requirements. The technological requirements and constraints, identified in Business Area Analysis, that will be considered by the design team.

Temporal event. The triggering of one or more processes at a predetermined time. These processes use only data that have been saved previously within the system.

Test harness. Software needed to test components of an application adequately.

Transaction. A series of manual steps and computer processing that enables an elementary process to be executed successfully.

INDEX